American Slavery

A Historical Collection of Primary Sources

Edited by
Jeffrey B. Harris

American Slavery: A Historical Collection of Primary Sources

Edited by Jeffrey B Harris

Copyright © February 2021 - Alpharetta, Georgia
Yonah Publishing

Cover- Illus. in: The Penitential Tyrant / Thomas Branagan. New-York: Printed by Samuel Wood, no. 362, Pearl-street, 1807.

Table of Contents

Excerpt from John Rolfe's letter to Edwin Sandys
1619
Jamestown, Virginia.

This is the source material used to suggest that the first African slaves in America arrived in 1619. This is evidence for slavery in Jamestown, but there were slaves before this in Spanish St. Augustine. Also, there is evidence of slaves accompanying Juan Ponce de Leon in 1513 through Florida. There are records of slaves in 1594 through Catholic parish marriage and baptism documents.

About the latter end of August, a Dutch man-of-war of the burden of a 160 tons arrived at Point Comfort, the Commander's name Captain Jope, his Pilot for the West Indies one Mr. Marmaduke, an Englishman. They met with the Treasure in the West Indies and determined to hold consort ship hitherward, but in their passage lost one the other. He brought not anything but 20 and odd Negroes, which the Governor and Cape Merchant bought for victuals (whereof

he was in great need as he pretended) at the best and easiest rate they could. He had a large and ample Commission from his Excellency to range and to take purchase in the West Indies.

Virginia. An Act Concerning Servants and Slaves.
October 1705. Selections

These are passed laws from the Virginia General Assembly in October of 1705. Many were already in place before this time, but the legislature added some new laws for slaves and indentured servants.

That all servants brought into this country without indenture, if the said servants be Christians and of Christian parentage, and above nineteen years of age, shall serve but five years; and if under nineteen years of age, 'till they shall become twenty-four years of age,and no longer. . . .
— That all servants imported and brought into this country by sea or land, who were not Christians in their native country, (except Turks and Moors in amity with her majesty, and others that can make due proof of their being free in England, or any other Christian country, before they were shipped, in order to transportation hither) shall be accounted and be slaves, and as such be here bought and sold notwithstanding a conversion to Christianity afterwards. . . .
— That all masters and owners of servants shall find and provide for their servants wholesome and competent diet, clothing, and lodging, by the discretion of the county court; and shall not, at any time,
give immoderate correction [excessive punishment]; neither shall at any time whip a Christian white servant naked without an order from a justice of the peace. . . .
— That all servants (not being slaves,) whether imported or become servants of their own accord here, or bound by any court or church-wardens, shall have their complaints received by a justice of the peace, who, if he find cause, shall bind the master over to answer the complaint at court. . . .

— That no negros, mulattos, or Indians, although Christians, or Jews, Moors, Mahometans [Muslims], or other infidels shall at any time purchase any Christian servant, nor any other, except of their own
complexion or such as are declared slaves by this act.
— That there shall be paid and allowed to every imported servant, not having yearly wages, at the time of service ended, by the master or owner of such servant, viz: To every male servant, ten bushels of
Indian corn, thirty shillings in money, or the value thereof in goods, and one well fixed musket or fuzee, of the value of twenty shillings, at least: and to every woman servant, fifteen bushels of Indian corn and forty shillings in money, or the value thereof in goods . . . .
— That in all cases of penal laws, whereby persons free are punishable by fine, servants shall be punished by whipping, after the rate of twenty lashes for every five hundred pounds of tobacco, or fifty shillings current money, unless the servant so culpable can and will procure some person or persons to pay the fine; in which case, the said servant shall be adjudged to serve such benefactor after the time by indenture, custom, or order of court, to his or her then present master or owner, shall be expired. . . .
— That whatsoever English or other white man or woman, being free, shall intermarry with a negro or mulatto man or woman, bond or free, shall by judgment of the county court be committed to prison
and there remain during the space of six months, without bail or main prize; and shall forfeit and pay ten pounds current money of Virginia, to the use of the parish. . . .
— And if any slave resist his master or owner or other person, by his or her order, correcting such slave,and shall happen to be killed in such correction, it shall not be accounted felony; but the master,
owner, and every such other person so giving correction shall be free and acquit of all punishment and accusation for the same, as if such accident had never happened; And also, if any negro, mulatto, or
Indian, bond or free, shall at any time lift his or her hand in opposition against any Christian, not being negro, mulatto, or Indian, he or she so offending shall, for every such offence proved by the oath of the
party, receive on his or her bare back thirty lashes, well laid on; cognizable by a justice of the peace for that county wherein such offense shall be committed. . . .
— That no slave go armed with gun, sword, club, staff, or other weapon, nor go from off the plantation and seat of land where such slave shall be appointed to live, without a certificate of leave in writing forso doing from his or her master, mistress, or overseer: And if any slave shall be found offending herein, it shall be lawful for any person or persons to apprehend and deliver such slave to the next
constable or head-borough, who is hereby enjoined and required, without further order or warrant, to give such slave twenty lashes on his or her bare back, well laid on, and so send him or her home. . . .
— That baptism of slaves does not exempt them from bondage; and that all children shall be bond or free, according to the condition of their mothers, and the particular directions of this act.

(1724) LOUISIANA'S CODE NOIR

This was a decree set by the French monarchy (King Louis XV) detailing slave codes and rules for free blacks in the colonies of the French empire. Although there is extensive coverage of slave behavior, this code applied to other areas of life. It made practicing the Jewish faith illegal and Catholicism was the only religion that could be practiced.

I. Decrees the expulsion of Jews from the colony.

II. Makes it imperative on masters to impart religious instruction to their slaves.

III. Permits the exercise of the Roman Catholic creed only. Every other mode of worship is prohibited.

IV. Negroes placed under the direction or supervision of any other person than a Catholic, are liable to confiscation.

V. Sundays and holidays are to be strictly observed. All negroes found at work on these days are to be confiscated.

VI. We forbid our white subjects, of both sexes, to marry with the blacks, under the penalty of being fined and subjected to some other arbitrary punishment. We forbid all curates, priests, or missionaries of our secular or regular clergy, and even our chaplains in our navy to sanction such marriages.
We also forbid all our white subjects, and even the manumitted or free-born blacks, to live in a state of concubinage with blacks. Should there be any issue from this kind of intercourse, it is our will that the person so offending, and the master of the slave, should pay each a fine of three hundred livres. Should said issue be the result of the concubinage of the master with his slave, said master shall not only pay the fine, but be deprived of the slave and of the children, who shall be adjudged to the hospital of the locality, and said slaves shall be forever incapable of being set free. But should this illicit intercourse have existed between a free black and his slave, when said free black had no legitimate wife, and should said black marry said slave according to the forms prescribed by the church, said slave shall be thereby set free, and the children shall also become free and legitimate ; and in such a case, there shall be no application of the penalties mentioned in the present article.

VII. The ceremonies and forms prescribed by the ordinance of Blois, and by the edict of 1639, for marriages, shall be observed both with regard to free persons and to slaves. But the consent of the father and mother of the slave is not necessary; that of the master shall be the only one required.

VIII. We forbid all curates to proceed to effect marriages between slaves without proof of the consent of their masters; and we also forbid all masters to force their slaves into any marriage against their will.

IX. Children, issued from the marriage of slaves, shall follow the condition of their parents, and shall belong to the master of the wife and not of the husband, if the husband and wife have different masters.

X. If the husband be a slave, and the wife a free woman, it is our will that their children, of whatever sex they may be, shall share the condition of their mother, and be as free as she, notwithstanding the servitude of their father; and if the father be free and the mother a slave, the children shall all be slaves.

XI. Masters shall have their Christian slaves buried in consecrated ground.

XII. We forbid slaves to carry offensive weapons or heavy sticks, under the penalty of being whipped, and of having said weapons confiscated for the benefit of the person seizing the same. An exception is made in favor of those slaves who are sent a hunting or a shooting by their masters, and who carry with them a written permission to that effect, or are designated by some known
mark or badge.

XIII. We forbid slaves belonging to different masters to gather in crowds either by day or by night, under the pretext of a wedding, or for any other cause, either at the dwelling or on the grounds of one of their masters, or elsewhere, and much less on the highways or in secluded places, under the penalty of corporal punishment, which shall not be less than the whip. In case of frequent offences of the kind, the offenders shall be branded with the mark of the flower de luce, and should there be aggravating circumstances, capital
punishment may be applied, at the discretion of our judges. We command all our subjects, be they officers or not, to seize all such offenders, to arrest and conduct them to prison, although there should be no judgment against them.

XIV. Masters who shall be convicted of having permitted or tolerated such gatherings as aforesaid, composed of other slaves than their own, shall be sentenced, individually, to indemnify their neighbors for the damages occasioned by said gatherings, and to pay, for the first time, a fine of thirty livres, and double that sum on the repetition of the offence.

XV. We forbid negroes to sell any commodities, provisions, or produce of any kind, without the written permission of their masters, or without wearing their known marks or badges, and any persons purchasing any thing from negroes in violence of this article, shall be sentenced to pay a fine of 1500 livres.

XVI, XVII, XVIII, XIX, provide at length for the clothing of slaves and for their subsistence.

XX. Slaves who shall not be properly fed, clad, and provided for by their masters, may give information thereof to the attorney-general of the Superior Council, or to all the other officers of justice of an inferior jurisdiction, and may put the written exposition of their wrongs into their hands ; upon which information, and even ex officio, should the information come from another quarter, the attorney-general shall prosecute said masters without charging any costs to the complainants. It is our will that this regulation be
observed in all accusations for crimes or barbarous and inhuman treatment brought by slaves against their masters.

XXI. Slaves who are disabled from working, either by old age, disease, or otherwise, be the disease incurable or not, shall be fed and provided for by their masters ; and in case they should have been abandoned by said masters, said slaves shall be adjudged to the nearest hospital, to which said masters shall be obliged to pay eight cents a day for the food and maintenance of each one of these slaves ; and for the payment of this sum, said hospital shall have
a lien on the plantations of the master.

XXII. We declare that slaves can have no right to any kind of property, and that all that they acquire, either by their own industry or by the liberality of others, or by any other means or title whatever, shall be the full property of their masters ; and the children of said slaves, their fathers and mothers, their kindred or other relations, either free or slaves, shall have no pretensions or claims thereto, either through testamentary dispositions or donations inter vi-vos ; which dispositions and donations we declare null and void, and also whatever promises they may have made, or whatever obligations they may have subscribed to, as having been entered into by persons incapable of disposing of any thing, and of participating to any contract.

XXIII. Masters shall be responsible for what their slaves have done by their command, and also for what transactions they have permitted their slaves to do in their shops, in the particular line of commerce with which they were intrusted ; and in case said slaves should have acted without the order or authorization of their masters, said masters shall be responsible only for so much as has turned to their profit; and if said masters have not profited by the doing or transaction of their slaves, the pcculium which the masters have permitted the slaves to own, shall be subjected to all claims against said slaves, after deduction made by the masters of what may be due to them ; and if said peculium should consist, in whole or in part, of merchandises in which the slaves had permission to traffic, the masters shall only come in for their share in common with the other creditors.

XXIV. Slaves shall be incapable of all public functions, and of being
constituted agents for any other person than their own masters, with powers to manage or conduct any kind of trade ; nor can they serve as arbitrators or experts; nor shall they be called to give their testimony either in civil or in criminal cases, except when it shall be a matter of necessity, and only in default of white people ; but in no case shall they be permitted to serve as witnesses either for or against their masters.

XXV. Slaves shall never be parties to civil suits, either as plaintiffs or
defendants, nor shall they be allowed to appear as complainants in criminal cases, but their masters shall have the right to act for them in civil matters, and in criminal ones, to demand punishment and reparation for such outrages and excesses as their slavee may havo sufforod from.

XXVI. Slaves may be prosecuted criminally, without their masters being made parties to the trial, except they should be indicted as accomplices; and said slaves shall be tried, at first, by the judges of ordinary jurisdiction, if
there be any, and on appeal, by the Superior Council, with the same rules, formalities, and proceedings observed for free persons, save the exceptions mentioned hereafter.

XXVII. The slave who, having struck his master, his mistress, or the husband of his mistress, or their children, shall have produced a bruise, or the shedding of blood in the face, shall suffer capital punishment.

XXVIII. With regard to outrages or acts of violence committed by slaves against free persons, it is our will that they be punished with severity, and even with death, should the case require it.

XXIX. Thefts of importance, and even the stealing of horses, mares, mules, oxen, or cows, when executed by slaves or manumitted persons, shall make the offender liable to corporal, and even to capital punishment, according to the circumstances of the case.

XXX. The stealing of sheep, goats, hogs, poultry, grain, fodder, peas, beans, or other vegetables, produce, or provisions, when committed by slaves, shall be punished according to the circumstances of the case ; and the judges may sentence them, if necessary, to be whipped by the public executioner, and branded with the mark of the flower de luce.

XXXI. In cases of thefts committed or damages done by their slaves, masters, besides the corporal punishment inflicted on their slaves, shall be bound to make amends for the injuries resulting from the acts of said slaves, unless they prefer abandoning them to the sufferer. They shall be bound so to make their choice, in three days from the time of the conviction of the negroes ; if not, this privilege shall be forever forfeited.

XXXII. The runaway slave, who shall continue to be so for one month from the day of his being denounced to the officers of justice, shall have his ears cut off, and shall be branded with the flower de luce on the shoulder : and on a second offence of the same nature, persisted in during one month from the day of his being denounced, he shall be hamstrung, and be marked with the flower de luce on the other shoulder. On the third offence, he shall suffer death.

XXXIII. Slaves, who shall have made themselves liable to the penalty of the whip, the flower de luce brand, and ear cutting, shall be tried, in the last resort, by the ordinary judges of the inferior courts, and shall undergo the sentence passed upon them without there being an appeal to the Superior Council, in confirmation or reversal of judgment, notwithstanding the article 26th of the present code, which shall be applicable only to those judgments in which the slave convicted is sentenced to be hamstrung or suffer death.

XXXIV. Freed or free-born negroes, who shall have afforded refuge in their houses to fugitive slaves, shall be sentenced to pay to the masters of said slaves, the sum of thirty livres a day for every day during which they shall have concealed said fugitives ; and all other free persons, guilty of the same offence, shall pay a fine of ten livres a day as aforesaid ; and should the freed or free-born negroes not be able to pay the fine herein specified, they shall be reduced to the condition of slaves, and be sold as such. Should the price of the sale exceed the sum mentioned in the judgment, the surplus shall be delivered to the hospital.

XXXV. We permit our subjects in this colony, who may have slaves concealed in any place whatever, to have them sought after by such persons and in such a way as they may deem proper, or to proceed themselves to such researches, as they may think best.

XXXVI. The slave who is sentenced to suffer death on the denunciation of his master, shall, when that master is not an accomplice to his crime, be appraised before his execution by two of the principal inhabitants of the locality, who shall be especially appointed by the judge, and the amount of said appraisement shall be paid to the master. To raise this sum, a proportional tax shall be laid on every slave, and shall be collected by the persons invested with that authority.

XXXVII. We forbid all the officers of the Superior Council, and all our other officers of justice in this colony, to take any fees or receive any perquisites in criminal suits against slaves, under the penalty, in so doing, of being dealt with as guilty of extortion.

XXXVIII. We also forbid all our subjects in this colony, whatever their condition or rank may be, to apply, on their own private authority, the rack to their slaves, under any pretence whatever, and to mutilate said slaves in any one of their limbs, or in any part of their bodies, under the penalty of the confiscation of said slaves ; and said masters, so offending, shall be liable to a criminal prosecution. We only permit masters, when they shall think that the case requires it, to put their slaves in irons, and to have them whipped with rods or ropes.

XXXIX. We command our officers of justice in this colony to institute criminal process against masters and overseers who shall have killed or mutilated their slaves, when in their power and under their supervision, and to punish said murder according to the atrocity of the circumstances; and in case the offence shall be a pardonable one, we permit them to pardon said masters and overseers without its being necessary to obtain from us letters patent of pardon. XL. Slaves shall he held in law as movables, and as such, they shall be part of the community of acquests between husband and wife ; they shall not be liable to be seized under any mortgage whatever; and they shall be equally divided among the co-heirs without admitting from any one of said heirs any claim founded on preciput or right of primogeniture, or dowry.

XLI, XLII. Are entirely relative to judicial forms and proceedings. XLIII.
Husbands and wives shall not be seized and sold separately when belonging to the same master : and their children, when under fourteen years of age, shall not be separated from their parents, and such seizures and sales shall be null and void. The present article shall apply to voluntary sales, and in case such sales should take place in violation of the law, the seller shall be deprived of the slave he has illegally retained, and said slave shall be adjudged to the purchaser without any additional price being required.

XLIV. Slaves, fourteen years old, and from this age up to sixty, who are settled on lands and plantations, and are at present working on them, shall not be liable to seizure for debt, except for what may be due out of the purchase money agreed to be paid for them, unless said grounds or plantations should also be distressed, and any seizure and judicial sale of a rea,l estate, without including the slaves of the aforesaid age, who are part of said estate, shall be deemed null and void.

XLV, XLVI, XLVII, XLVIII, XLIX. Are relative to certain formalities to be observed in judicial proceedings.

L. Masters, when twenty-five years old, shall have the power to manumit their slaves, cither by testamentary dispositions, or by acts inter vivos. But, as there may be mercenary masters disposed to set a price on the liberation of their slaves ; and whereas slaves, with a view to acquire the necessary means to purchase their freedom, may be tempted to commit theft or deeds of plunder, no person, whatever may he his rank and condition, shall be permitted to set free his slaves, without obtaining from the Superior Council a decree of permission to that effect ; which permission shall be granted without costs, when the motives for the setting free of said slaves, as specified in the petition of the master, shall appear legitimate to the tribunal. All acts for the emancipation of slaves, which, for the future, shall be made without this permission, shall be null ; and the slaves, so freed, shall not be entitled to their freedom ; they shall, on the contrary, continue to be held as slaves; but they shall be taken away from their former masters, and confiscated for the benefit of the India Company. LI. However, should slaves be appointed by their masters tutors to their children, said slaves shall be held and regarded as being thereby set free to all intents and purposes.

LII. We declare that the acts for the enfranchisement of slaves, passed according to the forms above described, shall be equivalent to an act of naturalization, when said slaves are not born in our colony of Louisiana, and they shall enjoy all the rights and privileges inherent to our subjects born in our kingdom or in any land or country under our dominion. We declare, therefore, that all manumitted slaves, and all free-born negroes, are incapable of receiving donations, either by testamentary dispositions, or by acts inter vivos from the whites. Said donations shall be null and void, and the objects so donated shall be applied to the benefit of the nearest hospital.

LIII. We command all manumitted slaves to show the pro foundest respect to their former masters, to their widows and children, and any injury or insult offered by said manumitted slaves to their former masters, their widows or children- shall be punished with more severity than if it had been offered to any other person. We, however, declare them exempt from the discharge Of all duties or services, and from the payment of all taxes or fees, or any thing else which their former masters might, in their quality of patrons, claim either in relation to their persons, or to their personal or real estate, either during the life or after the death of said manumitted slaves.

LIV. We grant to manumitted slaves the same rights, privileges, and immunities which are enjoyed by free-born persons. It is our pleasure that their merit in having acquired their freedom, shall produce in their favor, not only with regard to their persons, but also to their property, the same effects which our other subjects derive from the happy circumstance of their having been born free.
In the name of the King,
Bienville, De la Chaise.

Fazende, Bruslé

Travels Into the Inland Parts of Africa, By Francis Moore

This is an excerpt based off of the journal kept by Francis Moore, a clerk for the Royal African Company. He lived along the Gambia River for over four years and detailed the life there, its history and the slave trade.

I Left England, says Mr. Moore, in July 1730, on being appointed a writer in the service of the Royal African company, and on the 9th of November came to an anchor in the mouth of the Gambia. As we sailed up that river near the shore, the country appeared very beautiful, being for the most part woody; and between the woods were pleasant green rice grounds, which after the rice is cut, are stocked with cattle. On the 11th we landed at James's Island, which is situated in the middle of the river, that is here at least seven miles broad. This island lies about ten leagues from the river's mouth, and is about three quarters of a mile in circumference. Upon it is a square stone fort regularly built , with four bastions; and upon each are seven guns well mounted, that command the river all round: beside, under the walls of the fort facing the sea, are two round batteries, on each of which are four large cannon well mounted, that carry ball of 24 pounds weight, and between these are nine small guns mounted for salutes.

Beside the fort, there are several factories up the river, settled for the convenience of trade; but they are all under the direction of the governor and chief merchants of the fort. For this purpose the company have here about three or four sloops of about 30 tons each, and about the same number of long boats; some of which are constantly employed in fetching provisions and water from the main for the use of the garrison, and the rest are employed in carrying goods up to the factories, and bringing from them slaves, elephants teeth, and wax.

Soon after my arrival, I supped upon oysters that grew upon trees: this being somewhat remarkable, it may be thought worthy of an explanation. Down the river, where the water is salt, and near the sea, the river is bounded with trees called Mangroves; whose leaves being long and heavy, weigh the boughs into the water: to these leaves the young oysters fasten in great quantities, where they grow till they are very large, and then you cannot separate them from the tree, but are obliged to cut off the boughs with the oysters hanging on them, resembling ropes of onions.

On the 22d of February, one of the kings of Fonia came to the fort, and on his landing was saluted with five guns. He came to see the governor, or rather to ask for some powder and ball, in order to enable him to defend himself against some people with whom he was at war: he was a young man, very black, tall, and well set; was dressed in a pair of short yellow cotton-cloth breeches, and wore on his back a garment of the same cloth, made like a surplice: he had on his head a very large cap, to which was fastened part of a goat's tail, which is a customary ornament with the great men of this river; but he had no shoes nor stockings. He and his retinue came in a large canoe, holding about 16 people, all armed with guns and cutlasses. With him came two or three women, and the same number of Mundingo drums, which are about a yard long, and a foot or twenty inches diameter at the top, but less at the bottom; made out of a solid piece of wood, and covered at the widest end with the skin of a kid.

They beat upon them with the left hand, using only one drum-stick; and the women will dance very briskly to the sound. They staid at the fort all night, and then returned home, having nine guns fired at their going off.

It may be here proper to observe, that there are many different kingdoms on the banks of the Gambia, inhabited by several races of people, as Mundingoes, Jolloiffs, Pholeys, Floops, and Portuguese. The most numerous are called Mundingoes, as is likewise the country they inhabit: these are generally of a black colour, and well set. When this country was conquered by the Portuguese, about the year 1420, some of that nation settled in it, who have cohabited with these Mundingoes, till they are now very near as black as they: but as they still retain a sort of bastard Portuguese language, called Creole, and as they christen and marry by the help of a priest annually sent thither from St. Jago, one of the Cape de verde islands, they still esteem themselves Portuguese Christians, as much as if they were actually natives of Portugal; and nothing angers them more than to call them Negroes, that being a term they use only for slaves.

On the north-side of the river Gambia, and from thence in-land, are a people called Jolloiffs, whose country extends even to the river Senegal. These people are much blacker, and handsomer than the Mundingoes; for they have not the broad nose and thick lips peculiar to the Mundingoes and Floops.

In every kingdom and country on each side of the river are people of a tawney colour, called Pholeys, who resemble the Arabs, whose language most of them speak; for it is taught in their schools; and the koran, which is also their law, is in that language. They are more generally learned in the Arabic, than the people of Europe are in Latin; for they can most of them speak it, though they have a vulgar tongue
called Pholey. They live in hords or clans, build towns, and are not subject to any of the kings of the country, though they live in their territories; for if they are used ill in one nation, they break up their towns and move to another. They have chiefs of their own, who rule with such moderation, that every act of government seems rather an act of the people than of one man. This form of government is easily administered, because the people are of a good and quiet disposition, and so well instructed in what is just and right, that a man, who does ill, is the abomination of all.
In these countries the natives are not avaricious of lands; they desire no more than what they use, and as they do not plough with horses or cattle, they can use but very little.

The natives make no bread, but thicken liquids with the flour of the different grains. The maize they mostly use when green, parching it in the ear, when it eats like green peas. their rice they boil in the same manner as is practiced by the Turks; and make flour of the Guinea corn and mansaroke, as they also sometimes do of the two former species, by beating it in wooden mortars. The natives never bake cakes or bread for themselves, but those of their women who live among the Europeans learn to do both.

The Pholey are the greatest planters in the country, though they are strangers in it. They are very industrious and frugal, and raise much more corn and cotton than they consume, which they sell at reasonable rates; and are so remarkable for their hospitality, that the natives esteem it a blessing to have a Pholey town in the neighbourhood: beside, their behaviour has gained them such a reputation, that it is esteemed infamous for any one to treat them in an inhospitable manner.

The most general language used in these countries is the Mundingo; and whoever can speak it, may travel from the river's mouth up to the country of the Jencoes, or the merchants; a people so called, from their annually buying a great number of slaves there, and bringing them down to the lower parts of the river, to sell them to the Europeans; though I believe their country cannot be less than six weeks journey from James's Fort.

The next language mostly used here is called the Creole Portuguese; though I believe it would be scarce understood at Lisbon: it is, however, sooner learnt by Englishmen, than any other language used on the banks of this river, and is always spoken by the linguists or interpreters; and these two I learnt whilst in the river.

The Arabic is not only spoken by the Pholeys, but by most of the Mahometans in the river, though they are Mundingoes; and it is observed, that those who can write that language are not only very strict at their devotions three or four times a day; but are remarkably sober and abstemious in their manner of living.

On the 4th of April I went to Gillyfree, which is a large town, a little below James's fort, inhabited by Portuguese, Mundingoes, and some Mahometans, who have here a pretty little mosque. The English company have a factory here, pleasantly situated, facing the fort, and also some gardens that supply the fort with greens and fruit.

A native here took me to his house, and shewed me a great number of arrows, daubed over with a black mixture, said to be so venomous, that if the arrow did but draw blood it would be mortal, unless the person who made the mixture had a mind to cure it; for the man observed, that there were no poisonous herbs, whose effects might not be prevented by the application of other herbs.

On the 11th, came down the river a vessel commanded by captain Pyke, a separate trader, from Joar, loaded with slaves, among whom was a person of an elegant figure, named Job Ben Solomon, who was of the Pholey race, and son to the high priest of Bundo, in Foota, a place about ten days journey from Gillyfree. This person was travelling on the south side of the Gambia, with a servant, and about 20 or 30 head of cattle, which induced the king of a country a little within the land, to seize not only the cattle, but Job and his man, both of whom he sold for slaves to captain Pyke. The Pholeys, his humane countrymen, would have redeemed him; but they had the mortification to find that he was carried out of the river before they had notice of his being a slave; and captain Pyke sailed with him to Maryland. Job, who was a person of extraordinary abilities, and distinguished merit, was not so unhappy as he had reason to expect: but his adventures will be hereafter related, when I shall have occasion to mention his return to this country.
On the 29th, the governor and I set out for Vintain, where we arrived in three hours, though it lies about six leagues from James's fort. On our coming to the town, the Alcade, and all the principal inhabitants came to welcome us; and soon after came the prince, in whose dominions the town is situated.

The inhabitants are not very curious in their furniture, for the most that any of them have is a small chest for cloaths, a matt raised upon posts from the ground, to lie on; a jar to hold water, a callabash to drink it with; two or three wooden mortars, in which they pound their corn and rice; a basket which they use as a sieve, and two or three large callabashes, out of which they eat with their hands instead of spoons. They are not very careful of laying up store against a time of scarcity; but chuse rather to sell what they can, as upon occasion they can fast two or three days without eating; but then they are always smoaking tobacco, which is of their own growth.

Here are cameleons, and great numbers of crocodiles, which the natives kill and eat: they admire both them and their eggs, which I have frequently seen them eat, when they had young ones in them as long as my finger. This is one of their nicest dishes. Whilst I was here, I saw an ostrich, with a man riding upon its back, who was going down to the fort; it being a present to the governor, from one of our factors, who bought it at Fatatenda.

Soon after my arrival at Joar, the king of Barsally came thither, attended by three of his brothers, above 100 horsemen, and as many foot; and though he had a house of his own in the town, he insisted on lying at the factory. Mr. Roberts, Mr. Harrison, who were factors, and I, were all the English there. the king immediately took possession of Mr. Roberts's bed; and then having drank brandy till he was drunk, ordered Mr. Roberts to be held, while he himself took out of his pocket the keys of the storehouse, into which he and several of his people went, and took what they pleased: he searched chiefly for brandy; of which there happened to be but one anchor: he took that, and having drank till he was dead drunk, was put to bed. This anchor lasted him three days; and it was no sooner empty, than he went all over the house to seek for more. At last he entered a room, in which Mr. Harrison lay sick, and seeing there a case that contained six gallons and a half, that belonged to him and me, he ordered Mr. Harrison to get out of bed and open it: he, however, told him with great gravity, that there was nothing in it but some of the company's papers; and that it must not be opened; but the king was too well acquainted with liquor cases to be so easily deceived; and therefore ordered some of his men to hold Mr. Harrison in bed, while he himself took the key out of his breeches pocket. He then opened the chest, took out all the liquor, and was not sober while it lasted: but he often sent for Mr. Harrison and me to drink with him. At length it being all drank, he talked of going home; on which his people, and even his chief ministers, who were his general, and the keeper of his stores, amused themselves with taking whatever they liked, and had the assurance to open even chests and boxes. This we could not help, for what resistance could three men make against 200? What they took amounted to 20 l. sterling.

Sometimes the king would ride abroad, and take most of his attendants with him: but when he was gone we were plagued with the company of two of this brothers, who were, if possible, worse than his majesty. Once during his absence Boomey Haman Benda, one of these princes, laid hold of a mug of water, and pretending to drink, took a mouthful, and then setting the mug on the table, spurted the water in my face. Upon which, considering that if I suffered such insolence to pass unresented, it would render me liable to be continually insulted, I took the remainder of the water, and threw it into his breeches. Upon this he pulled out his knife, and endeavoured to stab me, but was prevented by his favorite attendant, who held his arm, and soon after represented to him the unhandsome manner in which he had treated me, and the provocation I had received to wet him. This made him so ashamed, that coming up to me, he laid himself down on the floor without his garment, took my foot, and placed it on his neck, and there lay till I desired him to rise: after which, no man appeared more my friend, no shewed greater willingness to oblige me.

This king, as well as all his attendants, are of the Mahometan religion, notwithstanding their being such drunkards; and this monster, when he is sober, even prays. His people, as well as himself, always wear white cloaths and white caps; and as they are exceeding black, this dress makes them look exceeding well.

This tyrant is tall, and so passionate, that when any of his men affront him, he makes no scruple of shooting them; and sometimes when he goes aboard a company's sloop at Cohone, where he usually resides, he inhumanly shews his dexterity by shooting at the canoes that pass by, frequently killing one or two men in a day. He has many wives, but never brings above two or three abroad at a time with him. Among his brothers, there are some to whom he seldom speaks, or permits to come into his company; and when they obtain his favour, they pull off their caps and garments, and throw dust upon their heads, as all except white men do, who come into the king's presence.
The dominions of this prince are very extensive, and are divided into several provinces, over which he appoints governors, called boomeys, who annually come to pay him homage.

At length the king and his guards, to our great joy, left the factory, in order to return to Cohone; but they first stript Mr. Roberts's chamber, and took away his cloaths and books, which last they offered to sell to a Mahometan priest; but he being a friend to Mr. Roberts, told them, he believed they were books in which he kept the account of his goods, and that to take them would inevitably ruin him: upon which they gave him leave to return them.

However, five months after, the king of Barsally paid us another visit, and staying about a week, during which he behaved much in the same manner as before, he and his attendants again left us; but some of them first broke open my bureau, and took out things to a considerable value; and the same fate attended Mr. Roberts: besides which they took a great quantity of the company's goods.

In the interval which passed between these two visits, I had been made factor, and had received orders to take charge of the factory of Joar: but I was unwilling to accept this office, as that factory was liable to many insults from a drunken monarch, void of every principle of justice, and destitute of the feeling of humanity. I therefore took an inventory of the goods the company had there, in January 1732, and taking a letter to the governor from Mr. Roberts, my collegue [sic], returned to James's Fort.

In March I returned to my factory: but Mr. Hugh Hamilton being sent up the river to settle a factory at Fatatenda, I was permitted to accompany him; and accordingly on the 9th on the 9th of April we left Joar, and proceeded in a sloop up the Gambia. The next day we arrived at Yanimarew, which is the pleasantest port on the whole river, the country being delightfully shaded with palm and palmetto trees. The company have here a small house, with a black factor, to purchase corn for the use of the fort.

On my arrival at Nackway, the natives welcomed me with the music of the balafeu, which, at about 100 yards distance, sounds something like a small organ. It is composed of about 20 pipes of very hard wood finely polished; which diminish by little and little, both in length and breadth, and are tied together by thongs of very fine leather. These thongs are twisted about small round wands, put between the pipes to keep them at a distance; and underneath the pipes are fastened 12 or 14 callabashes of different sizes. This instrument they play upon with two sticks, covered with a tin skin taken from the trunk of the palmetto tree, or with fine leather, to make the sound less harsh. Both men and women dance to this music, which they much admire, and are highly delighted to have a white man dance with them.

Having finished my business here, I returned to Yamyamacunda; and having continued there about three months, proceeded still farther up the river to Fatatenda. The Gambia is there as wide as the Thames at London-Bridge, and seemed very deep; but what is most extraordinary, the tide in the dry season rises three or four feet, though that place is 600 miles from the river's mouth.

On the 20th of November in the evening was a total eclipse of the moon; and the Mundingoes told me, the darkness was occasioned by a cat's putting her paw between the moon and the earth. The Mahometans in this country were singing and dancing the whole time, because they expect their prophet to come in an eclipse.

I stayed at Yamyamacunda, till the 5th of May, 1734; and was employed in the company's service in different parts of the river till the 13th of July following, when I was desired to come down to James's Fort: I was there on the 8th of August, when the Dolphin snow arrived, with four writers, and Job Ben Solomon, on board. We have already mentioned his being robbed and carried to Joar, where he was sold to captain Pyke, by whom he was carried to Maryland. Job was there sold to a planter, with whom he had lived about a twelvemonth, in all which time he had the happiness not to be struck by his master, and then the good fortune to have a letter of his own writing in the Arabic tongue conveyed to England. This letter coming to the hand of Mr. Oglethorp, he sent it to Oxford to be translated; which being done, it gave him such satisfaction, and inspired him with so good an opinion of the author, that he immediately sent orders to have him bought of his master. This happened a little before that gentleman's setting out for Georgia; and before his return from thence, Job arrived in England; where being brought to the acquaintance of Sir Hans Sloane, he was found to be a perfect master of the Arabic tongue, by his translating several manuscripts and inscriptions on medals. That learned antiquary recommended him to the duke of Montague, who being pleased with his genius and capacity, the agreeableness of his behaviour, and the sweetness of his temper, introduced him to court; where he was graciously received by the royal family and most of the nobility, who who honoured him with many marks of favour. The African company and the chief merchants of the city strove who should oftenest invite him to their tables. His good sense engaged their esteem; he freely discoursed on every subject, and attended the churches of the most celebrated divines. When he had been in England about 14 months, his ardent desire to see his native country made him press for his departure. He had wrote from England to the high priest his father, and earnestly longed to see him. Upon his setting out from England, he received many noble presents from queen Caroline, prince William, the duke of Montague, and the earl of Pembroke, several ladies of quality, Mr. Holden, and the royal African company; and the latter ordered all their agents to shew him the greatest respect.

On his arrival at James's Fort, Job desired that I would send a messenger to his country to let his friends know where he was. I spoke to one of the blacks whom he usually employed, to procure me a messenger, and he brought me a Pholey, who not only knew the high priest his father, but Job himself, and expressed great joy at seeing him safely returned from slavery; he being the only man, except one, ever known to come back to his country, after being once carried a slave out of it by white men. Job gave him the message himself, and desired that his father would not come down to him, observing that it was too far for him to travel; and that it was fit the young should go to the old, and not for the old to come to the young. He also sent some presents to his wives; and desired the man to bring his little one, who was his best beloved, down to him.

Job having a mind to go up to Joar, to talk with some of his countrymen, went along with me. We arrived at the creek of Damasensa; and having some old acquaintances at the town of that name, Job and I went in the yawl: in the way going up a narrow place for about half a mile, we saw several monkeys of a beautiful blue and red, which the natives told me never set their feet on the ground, but live entirely among the trees, leaping from one to another, at such great distances, as would appear improbable to any but an eyewitness.

In the evening as my friend Job and I were sitting under a great tree at Damasensa, there came six or seven of the very people, who, three years before, had robbed and made a slave of him, at about 30 miles distance from that place. Job, though naturally possessed of a very even temper, could not contain himself on seeing them: he was filled with rage and indignation, and was for attacking them with his broadsword and pistols, which he always took care to have about him. I had much ado to dissuade him from rushing upon them: but at length representing the ill consequences that would infallibly attend so rash an action, and the impossibility that either of us should escape alive, I made him lay aside the attempt, and persuading him to sit down, and pretending not to know them, to ask them questions about himself; which he accordingly did; and they told him the truth. At last he enquired how the king their master did? they replied that he was dead; and by farther inquiry we found that amongst the goods for which he sold Job to captain Pyke there was a pistol, which the king used commonly to wear slung by a string about his neck; and as they never carry arms without their being loaded, the pistol one day accidentally went off, and the balls lodging in his throat, he presently died. Job was so transported at the close of this story, that he immediately fell on his knees, and returned thanks to Mahomet for making him die by the very goods for which he sold him into slavery. The returning to me, he cried, "You see now, Mr. Moore, that God Almighty was displeased at this man's making me a slave, and therefore made him die by the very pistol for which he sold me: yet I ought to forgive him, because had not I been sold, I should neither have known any thing of the English tongue, nor have had any of the fine, useful, and valuable things, I have brought with me; nor have known that there is such a place in the world as England; nor such noble, good, and generous people as queen Caroline, prince William, the duke of Montague, the earl of Pembroke, Mr. Holden, Mr. Oglethorpe, and the royal African company."

After this Job went frequently with me to Cower, and several other places about the country. He always spoke very handsomely of the English; and what he said removed much of that horror the Pholeys felt for the state of slavery amongst them. For they before generally imagined, that all who were sold for slaves, were at least murdered, if not eaten, since none ever returned. His descriptions also gave them a high opinion of the power of England, and a veneration for the English, who traded amongst them. He sold some of the presents he brought with him for trading goods, with which he bought a woman slave, and two horses, which he designed to take with him to Bundo. He gave his countrymen a good deal of writing paper, a very valuable commodity amongst them, for the company had made him a present of several reams. He used frequently to pray; and he behaved with great affability and mildness to all, which rendered him extreamly popular.

The messenger not returning so soon as was expected, Job desired to go down to James's Fort, to take care of his goods; and I promised not only to send him word when the messenger came back, but to send other messengers, for fear the first should have miscarried.

At length the messenger returned with several letters, and advice that Job's father was dead; but had lived to receive the letters his son had sent him from England, which gave him the welcome news of his being redeemed from slavery, and an account of the figure he made in England: that one of Job's wives was married to another man; but that as soon as the new husband had heard of his return, he thought it adviseable to abscond; and that since Job's absence from his native country, there had been such a dreadful war, that the Pholeys there had not one cow left, though before Job's departure his countrymen were famed for their numerous herds. With this messenger came many of Job's old friends, whom he was exceeding glad to see; but notwithstanding the joy their presence gave him, he shed abundance of tears for the loss of his father, and the misfortunes of his country. He forgave his wife, and the man who had taken her; "For Mr. Moore, said he, she could not help thinking I was dead; for I was gone to a land from whence no Pholey ever yet returned; therefore neither she nor the man is to be blamed." During three or four days he conversed with his friends without any interruption except to sleep or eat.

As I have brought this account almost to the time of my leaving this country, it will be necessary to give a more particular description of it, with respect to the climate, the general customs of the natives, and the trade carried on there.

As the mouth of the Gambia lies in the latitude of 130; 20' north, and 150; 20' west longitude, there is no wonder that the climate is excessive hot; but the greatest heats are generally about the latter end of May, a fortnight or three weeks before the rainy season begins. The sun is perpendicular twice in the year, and the days are never longer from sun-rising to sun-set than 13 hours, nor even shorter than 11. What at first seemed to me strange, was that as soon as it grew light, the sun arose, and it no sooner set than it grew dark.

The rainy season commonly begins with the month of June, and continues till the latter end of September, or the beginning of October. The wind comes first and blows excessive hard, for the space of half an hour or more, before any rain falls, so that a vessel
may be suddenly surprised and overset by it: a person may however perceive the signs of its coming; for the clouds grow very black, and the lightenings darting from them, have an awful appearance. Both the thunder and the lightening are exceeding dreadful; the flashes succeeding each other so swiftly, as to render it continually light, while the thunder at the same time shakes the very ground. During the rain the air is generally cool: but the shower is no sooner over, than the sun breaks out excessive hot, which induces some people to cast off their cloaths, and lie down to sleep; but before they are awake, another tornado perhaps comes, when the cold strikes into their very bones, and gives them fits of illness, which to the Europeans are very fatal. During the rainy season the sea breezes seldom blow; but instead of them, easterly winds, which in the months of November, December, January, and February, generally blow very fresh, and sometimes the evenings and mornings are exceeding cold, and the middle of the day very hot.

Four months in the year are unhealthful, and very tedious to those who come from a colder climate; but a perpetual spring, in which you commonly see ripe fruit and blossoms on the same tree, makes some amends for that inconvenience. Beside, the heat of the air is frequently moderated by pleasant and refreshing breezes.

The Gambia is of such a length as to be navigable for sloops above 600 miles, the tides reaching so far from its mouth. The land on each side of this great and fine river is for the most part flat and woody about a quarter of a mile beyond its banks: and within that space are pleasant open grounds, on which the natives plant rice; and in the dry season it serves the cattle for pasture. Thus within land it is generally very woody; but near the towns there is always a large spot of ground cleared for corn. near the sea no hills are to be seen; but high up the river are lofty mountains. These are chiefly composed of iron stone, and though they are sometimes little else but a continued hard rock, they are full of trees, and serve greatly to beautify the face of the country.

In every kingdom there are several persons called lords of the soil, who have the property of all the palm and palmetto trees, so that none are allowed to draw any wine from them, without their knowledge and consent. Those who obtain leave to draw wine, give two days produce in a week, to the lord of the soil; and white men are obliged to make a small present to them, before they cut palmetto leaves, or grass, to cover their houses.

The palm is a fine straight tree that grows to a prodigious height, and out of it the natives extract a sort of white liquor like whey, called palm wine; by making an incision on the top of the trunk, to which they apply gourd bottles, and into these the liquor runs by means of a pipe made of leaves. This wine is very pleasant as soon as it is drawn, it being extraordinary sweet; but is apt to purge very much: however, in a day or two it ferments, and grows rough and strong like Rhenish wine; when not being at all prejudicial to the health, it is plentifully drank by all the negroes. It is very surprising to see how nimbly the natives will go up these trees, which are sometimes 60, 70, or 100 feet high, and the bark smooth. They have nothing to help them to climb, but a piece of the bark of a tree made round like a hoop, with which they enclose themselves and the tree; then fixing it under their arms, they set their feet against the tree, and their backs against the hoop, and go up very fast: but sometimes they miss their footing; or the bark on which they rest breaks or comes untied, when falling down, they lose their lives.

The people here, as in all other hot countries, marry their daughters very young; even some are contracted as soon as they are born, and the parents can never after break the match; but it is in the power
power of the man never to come and claim his wife; and yet without his consent she cannot marry another. Before a man takes his wife, he is obliged to pay her parents two cows, two iron bars, and 200 cola, a fruit that grows a great way within land: it is an exceeding good bitter, and much resembles a horse-chesnut with the skin off.

When a man takes home his wife, he makes a feast at his own house, to which all who please come without the form of an invitation. The bride is brought thither upon mens shoulders, with a veil over her face, which she keeps on till she has been in bed with her husband, during which the people dance and sing, beat drums, and fire muskets.

After his wife is brought to bed, she is not to lie with her husband for three years, if the child lives so long; for during that term the child sucks, and they are firmly persuaded that lying with their husbands would spoil their milk, and render the child liable to many diseases. The women alone are subject to all the mortifications attending so long an abstinence; for every man is allowed to take as many wives as he pleases: but if the wife is found false to her husband, she is liable to be sold for a slave. Upon any dislike, a man may turn off his wife, and make her take all her children with her; but if he has a mind to take any of them himself, he generally chuses such as are big enough to assist him in providing for his family. He has even the liberty of coming several years after they have parted, and taking from her any of the children he had by her. But if a man is disposed to part with a wife who is pregnant, he cannot oblige her to go till she is delivered.

The women are kept in the greatest subjection; and the men, to render their power as compleat as possible, influence their wives to give them an unlimited obedience, by all the force of fear and terror. For this purpose the Mundingoes have a kind of image eight or nine feet high, made of the bark of trees, dressed in a long coat, and crowned with a whisp of straw. This is called a Mumbo Jumbo; and whenever the men have any dispute with the women, this is sent for to determine the contest, which is almost always done in favour of the men. One who is in the secret, conceals himself under the coat, and bringing in the image, is the oracle on these occasions. No one is allowed to come armed into his presence. When the women hear him coming, they run away and hide themselves; but if you are acquainted with the person concealed in the Mumbo Jumbo, he will send them all to come, make them sit down, and afterward either sing or dance, as he pleases; and if any refuse to come, he will send for, and whip them. Whenever any one enters into this society, they swear in the most solemn manner never to divulge the secret to any woman, or to any person that is not entered into it: and to preserve the secret inviolable, no boys are admitted under 16 years of age. The people also swear by the Mumbo Jumbo; and the oath is esteemed irrevocable. There are very few towns of any note that have not one of these objects of terror, to frighten the poor women into obedience.

About the year 1727, the king of Jagra having a very inquisitive woman to his wife, was so weak as to disclose to her this secret; and she being a gossip, revealed it to some other women of her acquaintance. This at last coming to the ears of some who were no friends to the king, they, dreading lest if the affair took vent, it should put a period to the subjection of their wives, took the coat, put a man into it, and going to the king's town, sent for him out, and taxed him with it: when he not denying it, they sent for his wife, and killed them both on the spot. Thus the poor king died for his complaisance to his wife, and she for her curiosity.

The women pay such respect to their husbands, that when a man has been a day or two from home his wives salute him on their knees; and in the same posture they always give him water to drink.
When a child is born they dip him over head and ears in cold water three or four times in a day; and as soon as he is dry, rub him over with palm oil, particularly the back-bone, the small of the back, the elbows, the neck, knees, and hips. When they are born they are of an olive colour, and sometimes do not turn black till they are a month or two old.

I do not find that they are here born with flat noses; but the mothers, when they wash the children, press down the upper part of the nose: for large breasts, thick lips, and broad nostrils, are esteemed extreamly beautiful. One breast is generally larger than the other.

About a month afterward they name the child, which is done by shaving its head, and rubbing it over with oil; and a short time before the rainy season, they circumcise a great number of boys, of about 12 or 14 years of age, after which the boys put on a peculiar habit; the dress of each kingdom being different. From the time of their circumcision to that of the rains, they are allowed to commit what outrages they please, without being called to account for them; and when the first rain falls, the term of this licentiousness being expired, they put on their proper habit. The people are naturally very jocose and merry, and will dance to a drum or ballafeu, sometimes 24 hours together, now and then dancing very regularly, and at other times using very odd gestures, striving always to outdo each other in nimbleness and activity.

The behaviour of the natives to strangers is really not so disagreeable as people are apt to imagine; for when I went through any of their towns, they almost all came to shake hands with me, except some of the women, who having never before seen a white man, ran away from me as fast as they could, and would not by any means be persuaded to come near me. Some of the men invited me to their houses, and brought their wives and daughters to see me; who then sat down by me, and always found something to wonder at and admire, as my boots, spurs, cloaths, or wig.

Some of the Mundingoes have many slaves in their houses; and in these they pride themselves. They live so well and easily, that it is sometimes difficult to know the slaves from their masters and mistresses; they being frequently better cloathed, especially the females, who have sometimes coral, amber, and silver, about their wrists, to the value of 20 or 30 l. sterling.

In almost every town they have a kind of drum of a very large size, called a tangtong, which they only beat at the approach of an enemy, or on some very extraordinary occasion, to call the inhabitants of the neighbouring towns to their assistance; and this in the nigh-time may be heard six or seven miles.

There was a custom in this country which is not thoroughly repealed, that whatever commodity a man sells in the morning, he may, if he repents his bargain, go and have it returned to him again, on his paying back the money any time before the setting of the sun the same day. This custom is still in force very high up the river; but below it is pretty well worn out.

Whenever any factories are settled, it is customary to put them, and the persons belonging to them, under the charge of the people of the nearest large town, who are obliged to take care of it, and to let none impose upon the white men, or use them ill; and if any body is abused, he must apply to the alcalde, the head man of the town, who will see that justice is done him. This man is, up the river, called the white man's king; and has beside very great power. Almost every town has two common fields, one for their corn and the other for their rice, and he appoints the labour of the people: he sees that the men work in the corn fields, and the women and girls in the rice grounds, and afterward divides the crop among them. He likewise decides all quarrels, and has the first voice in all conferences relating to any thing belonging to the town.

The trade of the natives consists in gold, slaves, elephants teeth, and bees-wax. The gold is finer than sterling, and is brought in small bars, big in the middle, and turned round into rings, from 10 to 40 s. each. The merchants who bring this, and other inland commodities, are blacks of the Mundingo race, called Joncoes, who say, that the gold is not washed out of the sand, but dug out of mines in the mountains, the nearest of which is 20 days journey up the river. In the country where the mines are, they say there are houses built with stone, and covered with terras; and that the short cutlasses and knives of good steel, which they bring with them, are made there.

The same merchants bring down elephants teeth,and in some years slaves to the amount of 2000, most of whom they say are prisoners of war; and bought of the different princes by whom they are taken. The way of bringing them is, by tying them by the neck with leather thongs, at about a yard distance from each other, 30 or 40 in a string, having generally a bundle of corn, or an elephant's tooth upon each of their heads. In their way from the mountains they travel through extensive woods, where they cannot for some days get water; they therefore carry in skin bags enough to support them for that time. I cannot be certain of the number of merchants who carry on this trade; but there may perhaps be about 100 who go up into the inland country with the goods, which they buy from the white men, and with them purchase, in various countries, gold, slaves, and elephants teeth. They use asses, as well as slaves, in carrying their goods, but no camels or horses.

Beside the slaves brought down by the negro merchants, there are many bought along the river, who are either taken in war like the former, or condemned for crimes, or stolen by the people: but the company's servants never buy any which they suspect to be of the last sort, till they have sent for the alcalde, and consulted with him. Since this slave trade has been used, all punishments are changed into slavery; and the natives reaping advantage from such condemnations, they strain hard for crimes, in order to obtain the benefit of selling the criminal: hence not only murder, adultery, and theft, are here punished by selling the malefactor; but every trifling crime is also punished in the same manner. Thus at Cantore, a man seeing a tyger eating a deer, which he himself had killed and hung up near his house, fired at the tyger, but unhappily shot a man: when the king had not only the cruelty to condemn him for this accident; but had the injustice and inhumanity to order also his mother, his three brothers, and his three sisters, to be sold. They were brought down to me at Yamyamacunda, when it made my heart ache to see them; but on my refusing to make this cruel purchase, they were sent father down the river, and sold to some separate traders at Joar, and the vile avaricious king had the benefit of the goods for which they were sold.

Indeed the cruelty and villainy of some of these princes can scarcely be conceived. Thus, whenever the king of Barsally, some of whose villainies I have already mentioned, wants goods or brandy, he sends to the governor of James's Fort, to desire him to send a sloop there with a proper cargo; which is readily complied with. Mean while, the king goes and ransacks some of his enemies towns, and seizing the innocent people, sells them to the factors in the sloop for such commodities as he wants, as brandy, rum, guns, gunpowder, ball, pistols, and cutlasses, for his attendants and soldiers with coral and silver for his wives and concubines: but in case he is not at war with any neighbouring king, he then falls upon one of his own towns, which are very numerous, and uses them in the same manner, selling those for slaves, whom he is bound by every obligation to protect.

Several of the natives of these countries have many slaves born in their families. This there is a whole village near Brucoe of 200 people, who are the wives, slaves, and children of one man. And though in some parts of Africa they sell the slaves born in the family; yet this is here thought extreamly wicked; and I never heard but of one person who ever sold a family slave, except for such crimes as would have authorised its being done, had he been free. Indeed, if there are many slaves in the family, and one of them commits a crime, the master cannot sell him without the joint consent of the rest: for if he does, they will run away to the next kingdom, where they will find protection.

Ivory, or elephants teeth, is the next principal article of commerce. These are obtained either by hunting and killing the beasts, or are picked up in the woods. This is a trade used by all the nations hereabouts; for whoever kills an elephant, has the liberty of selling him and his teeth. But those traded for in this river are generally bought from a good way within the land. The largest tooth I ever saw weighed 130 pounds.

The fourth branch of trade consists in bees-wax. The Mundingoes make beehives of straw shaped like ours, and fixing to each a bottom board, in which is a hole, for the bees to go in and out, hang them on the boughs of trees. They smother the bees in order to take the combs, and pressing out the honey, of which they make a kind of metheglin, boil up the wax with water, strain it, and press it through hair cloths into holes made in the ground.

At length, on the 8th of April 1735, having delivered up the company's effects to Mr. James Conner, I embarked on board the company's sloop. Among other persons, Job came down with me to the sloop, and parted with me with tears in his eyes; at the same time giving me letters to the duke of Montague, the royal African company, Mr. Oglethorpe, and several other gentlemen in England, telling me to give his love and duty to them, and to acquaint them, that as he designed to learn to write the English tongue, he would, when he was master of it, send them longer epistles. He desired me, that as I had lived with him almost ever since he came there, I would let his grace and the other gentlemen know what he had done; and that he was going to the gum forest, and would endeavour to produce so good an understanding between the company and the Pholeys, that he did not doubt but that the English would procure the gum trade: adding, that he would spend his days in endeavouring to do good to the English, by whom he had been redeemed from slavery, and from whom he had received innumerable favours.

Soon after he returned on shore, while I sailed to England; and at length, on the 13th of July, landed at Deal.

Memoir of John Woolman
Considerations on the Keeping of Negroes.

John Woolman was a Quaker abolitionist that wrote this essay in 1754, at the onset of the French and Indian War. He believed that slavery went against the ideas of Christianity and he set out on a crusade to convince others of this evil practice.

As many times there are different motives to the same action; and one does that from a generous heart, which another does for selfish ends ; the like may be said in this case.

There are various circumstances among those that keep negroes, and different ways by which they fall under their care; and I doubt not, there are many well disposed persons amongst them who desire rather to manage...in this difficult matter, than to make gain of it.

But the general disadvantage which these poor negroes lie under in an enlightened Christian country, having often filled me with real sadness, I now think it my duty, through ... aid, to offer some thoughts thereon to the consideration of others.

When we remember that all nations are of one blood, (Gen. lii. 20,) that in this world we are but sojourners, that we are subject to the like afflictions and infirmities of body, the like disorders and frailties in mind, the like temptations, the same death, and the same judgment, and that the all-wise Being is Judge and Lord over us all, it seems to raise an idea of general brotherhood, and a disposition easy to be touched with a feeling of each other's afflictions : but when we forget those things, and look chiefly at our outward circumstances, in this and some ages past, constantly retaining in our minds the distinction between us and them, with respect to our knowledge and improvement in things Divine, natural and artificial, our breasts being apt to be filled with fond notions of superiority, there is danger of erring in our conduct toward them.

We allow them to be of the same species with ourselves ; odds is, we are in a higher station, and enjoy greater favor than they. And when it is thus that our heavenly Father e doweth some of his children with distinguished gifts, they intended for good ends ; but if those thus gifted are thereby hated Tip above their brethren, not considering themselves as debtors to the weak, nor behaving themselves as faithful stewards, none who judge impartially can suppose them free from ingratitude.

When a people dwell under the liberal distribution of favours from heaven, it behoves them carefully to inspect their ways, and consider the purposes for which those favours are bestowed, lest, through forgetfulness of God and misusing his gifts, they incur his heavy displeasure, whose judgments are just and equal, who exalteth and humbleth to the dust, as he seeth meet.

It appears, by Holy Record, that men under high favours have been apt to err in their opinions concerning others. Thus Israel, according to the description of the prophet, Isa. lxv. 5, when exceedingly corrupted and degenerated, yet remembered they were the chosen people of God ; and could say, " Stand by thyself, come not near me, for I am hoHer than thou." That this was no chance language, but their common opinion of other people, more fully appears, by considering the circumstances which attended when God was beginning to fulfil his precious promises concerning the gathering of the Gentiles.

The Most High, in a vision, undeceived Peter, first prepared his heart to believe, and at the house of Cornelius showed him of a certainty that God is no respecter of persons.

The effusion of the Holy Ghost upon a people, with whom they, the Jewish Christians, would not so much as eat, was strange to them. All they of the circumcision were astonished to see it; and the apostles and brethren of Judea contended with Petoi about it, till he having rehearsed the whole matter, and fully shown that the Father's love was unlimited, they are thereat struck with admiration, and cry out, " Then hath God also to the Gentiles granted repentance unto life."

The opinion of peculiar favours being confined to them, was deeply rooted, or else the above instance had been less strange to them, for these reasons : First, They were generally acquainted with the writings of the prophets, by whom this time was repeatedly spoken of, and pointed at. Secondly, Our blessed Lord shortly before expressly said, " I have other sheep, not of this fold, them also must I bring," &c. Lastly, His words to them after his resurrection, at the very time of his ascension, "Ye shall be witnesses to me, not only in Jerusalem, Judea, and Samaria,
but to the uttermost parts of the earth."

These concurring circumstances, one would think, might have raised a strong expectation of seeing such a time ; yet when it came, it proved matter of offence and astonishment.

To consider mankind otherwise than brethren, to think favours are peculiar to one nation, and to exclude others, plainly supposes a darkness in the understanding : for as God's love is universal, so where the mind is sufficiently influenced by it, it begets a like- ness of itself, and the heart is enlarged towards all men. Again, to conclude a people forward, perverse, and worse by nature than others, who ungratefully receive favours, and apply them to bad ends, will excite a behaviour toward them unbecoming the excellence of true religion.

To prevent such an error, let us calmly consider their circumstance : and the better to do it, make their case ours. Suppose then that our ancestors and we had been exposed to constant servitude, in the more servile and inferior employments of life ; that we had been destitute of the help of reading and good company; that amongst ourselves we had had but few wise and pious instructors ; that the religious amongst our superiors seldom too notice of us ; that while others in ease had plentifully heaped up the fruit of our labour, we had received barely enough to relieve nature ; and being wholly at the command of others, had generally been treated as a contemptible, ignorant part of mankind ; should we, in that case, be less abject than they now are ! Again, if oppression be so hard to bear, that a wise man is made mad by it, Eccl. vii. 7, then a series of oppressions, altering the behaviour and manners of a people, is what may reasonably be expected.

When our property is taken contrary to our mind, by means
appearing to us unjust, it is only through Divine influence, and the enlargement of heart from thence proceeding, that we can love our reputed oppressors. If the negroes fall short in this, an uneasy, if not a disconsolate disposition will be awakened, and remain like seeds in their minds, producing sloth and other habits which appear odious to us ; and with which, had they been free men, they would not perhaps have been chargeable. These, and other circumstances, rightly considered, will lessen the too great disparity which some make between us and them.

Integrity of heart has appeared in some of them ; so that if we continue in the word of Christ, and our conduct towards them be seasoned with his love, we may hope to see the good effect of it.

This, in a good degree, is the case with some into whose hands they have fallen ; hut that too many treat them otherwise, not seeming conscious of any neglect, is, alas ! too evident.

When self-love presides in our minds, our opinions are biassed in our own favour ; and in this condition, being concerned with a people so situated that they have no voice to plead their own
cause, there is danger of using ourselves to an undisturbed ..., until, by long custom, the mind becomes reconciled with it, and the judgment itself infected.

To apply humbly to God for wisdom, that we may thereby be enabled to see things as they are, and as they ought to be, is very needful. Hereby the hidden things of darkness may be brought to light, and the judgment made clear : we shall then consider mankind as brethren. Though different degrees and a variety of qualifications and abilities, one dependent on another, be admitted, yet high thoughts will be laid aside, and all men treated as becometh the sons of one father, agreeably to the doctrine of Christ Jesus.

"He hath laid down the best criterion, by which mankind ought to judge of their own conduct, and others judge for them of theirs, one towards another, viz. ' Whatsoever ye would that men should do unto you, do ye even so to them.' I take it, that all men by nature are equally entitled to the equity of this rule, and under the indispensable obligations of it. One man ought not to look upon another man or society of men as so far beneath him that he should not put himself in their place, in all his actions towards them, and bring all to this test, viz. How should I approve of this conduct, were I in their circumstance, and they in mine ?"

This doctrine being of a moral unchangeable nature, hath been likewise inculcated in the former dispensation; "If a stranger sojourn with thee in your land, ye shall not vex him ; but the stranger that dwelleth with you shall be as one born amongst 3'ou, and thou shalt love him as thyself." Had these people come voluntarily and dwelt amongst us, to call them strangers would be proper ; and their being brought by force, with regret and a languishing mind, may well raise compassion in a heart rightly disposed : but there is nothing in such treatment which, upon a wise and judicious consideration, will in any way lessen their right to be treated as strangers. If the treatment which many of them meet with be rightly examined, and compared with those precepts, "Thou shalt not vex him nor oppress him ; he shall be as one born amongst you, and thou shalt love him as thyself," there will appear an important difference between them.

It may be objected that there is the cost of purchase, and risk of their lives to them who possess them, and therefore it is needful that they make the best use of their time. In a practice just and reasonable, such objections may have weight ; but if the work be wrong from the beginning, there is little or no force in them. If I purchase a man who has never forfeited his liberty, the natural right of freedom is in him ; and shall I keep him and his posterity in servitude and ignorance ? " How should I approve of this conduct, were I in his circumstances, and he in mine ?" It may be thought, that to treat them as we would willingly be treated, our gain by them would be inconsiderable : and it were, in divers respects, better that there were none in our country.

We may further consider, that they are now amongst us, and people of our nation were the cause of their being here ; that whatsoever difficulty accrues thereon, we are justly chargeable with, and to bear all inconveniences attending it with a serious and weighty concern of mind to do our duty by them, is the best we can do. To seek a remedy by continuing the oppression, because we have power to do it, and see others do it, will, I apprehend, not be doing as we would be done by.

How deeply soever men are involved in difficulties, sincerity of heart, and upright walking before God, freely submitting to his providence, is the most sure remedy. He only is able to relieve, not only persons, but nations in their greatest calamities.

To act continually with integrity of heart, above all narrow or selfish motives, is a sure token of our being partakers of that salvation which " God hath appointed for wails and bulwarks," and is, beyond all contradiction, a more happy situation than can ever be promised by the utmost reach of art and power united, not proceeding from heavenly wisdom.

A supply to nature's lawful wants, joined with a peaceful, humble mind, is the truest happiness in this life ; and if we arrive at this, and continue to walk in the path of the just, our case will be truly happy. Though herein we may part with, or miss of the glaring show of riches, and leave our children little else but wise instructions, a good example, and the knowledge of some honest employment ; these, with the blessing of Providence, are sufficient for their happiness, and are more likely to prove so, than laying up treasures for them, which are often rather a snare than any real benefit ; especially to those who, instead of being exampled to temperance, are in all things taught to prefer the getting of riches, and to eye the temporal distinctions they give, as the principal business of this hfe. These readily overlook the true happiness of man, which results from the enjoyment of all things in the fear of God, and miserably substituting an inferior good, dangerous in the acquiring and uncertain in the fruition, they are subject to many disappointments, and every sweet carries its sting.

It is the conclusion of our blessed Lord and his apostles, as appears by their lives and doctrines, that the highest delights of sense, or most pleasing objects visible, ought ever to be accounted infinitely inferior to that real intellectual happiness, suited to man in his primitive innocence, and now to be found in true renovation of mind ; and that the comforts of our present life, the things most grateful to us, ought always to be received with temperance, and never made the chief objects of our desire, hope, or love ; but that our whole heart and affections be principally looking to that "city, which hath foundations, whose maker and builder is God." Did we so improve the gifts bestowed on us, that our children might have an education suited to these doctrines, and our example to confirm it, we might rejoice in hope of their being heirs of an inheritance incorruptible.

This inheritance, as Christians, we esteem the most valuable ; and how then can we fail to desire it for our children ? O that we were consistent with ourselves, in pursuing the means necessary to obtain it !

It appears by experience, that where children are educated in fulness, ease, and idleness, evil habits are more prevalent than is common amongst such who are prudently employed in the necessary affairs of hfe. If children are not only educated in the way of so great temptation, but have also the opportunity of lording it over their fellow-creatures, and being masters of men in their childhood, how can we expect otherwise than that their tender minds will be possessed with thoughts too high for them ; which gaining strength by continuance, will prove like a slow current, gradually separating them from or keeping from acquaintance with that humility and meekness in which alone lasting happiness can be enjoyed.

Man is born to labour, and experience abundantly showeth, that it is for our good : but where the powerful lay the burden on the inferior, without affording a Christian education, and suitable opportunity of improving the mind, and a treatment which we, in their case, should approve, in order that themselves may live at ease, and fare sumptuously, and lay up riches for their posterity; this seems to contradict the design of Providence, and, I doubt not, is sometimes the effect of a perverted mind ; for while the life of one is made grievous by the rigour of another, it entails misery on both.

Amongst the manifold works of Providence, displayed in the different ages of the world, these which follow, with many others, may afford instruction.

Abraham was called of God to leave his country and kindred, to sojourn amongst strangers. Through famine, and danger of death, he was forced to flee from one kingdom to another ; yet, at length, he not only had assurance of being the father of many nations, but became a mighty prince. (Gen. xxiii. 6.)

Remarkable were the dealings of God with Jacob in a low estate; the just sense he retained of them after his advancement, appears by his words : " I am not worthy of the least of all thy mercies."

The numerous afflictions of Joseph are very singular; the particular providence of God therein, no less manifest: he at length became governor of Egypt, and famous for wisdom and virtue.

The series of troubles which David passed through, few amongst us are ignorant of; and yet he afterwards became as one of the great men of the earth.

Some evidences of the Divine wisdom appear in those things, in that such who are intended for high stations, have first been very low and dejected, that Truth might be sealed on their hearts; and that the characters there imprinted by bitterness and adversity, might in after years remain, suggesting compassionate ideas, and, in their prosperity, quicken their regard to those in the like condition. This yet further appears in the case of Israel ; who were well acquainted with grievous sufferings, a long and rigorous servitude ; and then, through many notable events, were made chief amongst the nations. To them we find a repetition of precepts to the purpose above said : though, for ends agreeable to infinite wisdom, they were chosen as a peculiar people for a time ; yet the Most High acquaints them, that his love is not confined, but extends to the stranger ; and to excite their compassion, reminds them of times past, "Ye were strangers in the land of Egypt." Again, "Thou shalt not oppress a stranger, for ye
know the heart of a stranger, seeing ye were strangers in the
land of Egypt."

If we call to mind our beginning, some of us may find a time, wherein our fathers were under afflictions, reproaches, and manifold sufferings.

Respecting our progress in this land, the time is short since our beginning was small and number few, compared with the native inhabitants. He that sleeps not by day nor night, hath watched over us, and kept us as the apple of his eye. His Almighty arm hath been round about us, and saved us from dangers.

The wilderness and solitary deserts in which our fathers passed the days of their pilgrimage, are now turned into pleasant fields ; and while many parts of the world have groaned under the hea\y calamities of war, our habitation remains quiet, and our land fruitful.

When we trace back the steps we have trodden, and see how the Lord hath opened a way in the wilderness for us, to the wise it will easily appear, that all this was not done to be buried in oblivion, but to prepare a people for more fruitful returns ; and the remembrance thereof ought to humble us in prosperity, and excite in us a Christian benevolence towards our inferiors.

If we do not consider these things aright, but through a stupid indolence, conceive views of interest separate from the general good of the great brotherhood, and, in pursuance thereof, treat our inferiors with rigour, to increase our wealth and gain riches for our children; "What then shall we do when God riseth up? and when he visited, what shall we answer him ? did not he that made us, make them? and did not one fashion us?"

To our great Master we stand or fall, to judge or condemn us as is most suitable to his wisdom or authority ; my inclination is to persuade, and entreat, and simply give hints of my way of thinking.

If the Christian religion be considered, both respecting its doctrines and the happy influence which it hath on the minds and manners of all real Christians, it looks reasonable to think, that the miraculous manifestation thereof to the world is a kindness beyond expression.

Are we the people thus favoured ? Are we they whose minds are opened, influenced, and governed by the Spirit of Christ, and thereby made sons of God ? Is it not a fair conclusion, that we, like our heavenly Father, ought in our degree to be active in the same great cause of the eternal happiness of, at least, our whole families, and more, if thereto capacitated ?

If we, by the operation of the Spirit of Christ, become heirs with him in the kingdom of his Father, and are redeemed from the alluring counterfeit joys of this World, and the joy of Christ remain in us; to suppose that one in this happy condition can, for the sake of earthly riches, not only deprive his fellow-creatures of the sweetness of freedom, which, rightly used, is one of the greatest temporal blessings, but therewith neglect using pro- per means for their acquaintance with the Holy Scriptures, and the advantage of true religion, seems at least a contradiction to reason.

Whoever rightly advocates the cause of some, thereby promotes the good of all. The state of mankind was harmonious in the beginning, and though sin hath introduced discord, yet through the wonderful love of God in Christ Jesus our Lord, the way is open for our redemption, and means appointed to restore us to primitive harmony. That if one suffer by the unfaithfulness of another, the mind, the most noble part of him that occasions the discord, is thereby alienated from its true and real happiness.

Our duty and interest are inseparably limited, and when we neglect or misuse our talents, we necessarily depart from the heavenly fellowship, and are in the way to the greatest of evils.

Therefore to examine and prove ourselves, to find what harmony the power presiding in us bears with the Divine nature, is a duty not more incumbent and necessary, than it would be beneficial.

In Holy Writ the Divine Being saith of himself, " I am the Lord, which exercise loving-kindness, judgment and righteousness in the earth ; for in these things I delight, saith the Lord." Again, speaking in the way of man, to show his compassion to Israel, whose wickedness had occasioned a calamity, and then being humbled under it, it is said, " His soul was grieved for their miseries." If we consider the life of our blessed Saviour, when on earth, as it is recorded by his followers, we shall find that one uniform desire for the eternal and temporal good of mankind, discovered itself in all his actions.

If we observe men, both apostles and others, in many different ages, who have really come to the unity of the Spirit, and the fellowship of the saints, there still appears the like disposition; and in them the desire for the real happiness of mankind has out-balanced the desire of ease, liberty, and, many times, of hfe itself.

If, upon a true search, we find that our natures are so far renewed, that to exercise righteousness and loving-kindness, according to our ability, towards all men, without respect of persons, is easy to us, or is our delight ; if our love be so orderly and regular, that he who doeth the will of our Father, who is in heaven, appears in our view to be our nearest relation, our brother, and sister, and mother ; if this be our case, there is a good foundation to hope, that the blessing of God will sweeten our treasures during our stay in this life, and that our memory will be savoury, when we are entered, into rest.

To conclude. It is a truth most certain, that a life guided by wisdom from above, agreeably with justice, equity and mercy, is throughout consistent and amiable, and truly beneficial to society; the serenity and calmness of mind in it, affords an unparalleled comfort in this life, and the end of it is blessed.

And it is no less true, that they who in the midst of high favours remain ungrateful, and under all the advantages that a Christian can desire, are selfish, earthly and sensual, do miss the true fountain of happiness, and wander in a maze of dark anxiety, where all their treasures are insufficient to quiet their minds ; hence, from an insatiable craving, they neglect doing good with what they have acquired, and too often add oppression to vanity, that they may compass more.

" O that they were wise, that they understood this, that they
would consider their latter end !"

Lord Dunmore's Proclamation
1775

Dunmore's Proclamation set the stage for slave escapes and rebellions during the American Revolution. This was a military strategy, not a moral one, to cause disarray in the colonies at the onset of the war.

As I have ever entertained Hopes that an Accommodation might have taken Place between Great Britain and this Colony, without being compelled, by my Duty, to this most disagreeable, but now absolutely necessary Step, rendered so by a Body of armed Men, unlawfully assembled, firing on his Majesty's Tenders, and the Formation of an Army, and that Army now on their March to attack his Majesty's Troops, and destroy the well-disposed Subjects of this Colony: To defeat such treasonable Purposes, and that all such Traitors, and their Abettors, may be brought to Justice, and that the Peace and good Order of this Colony may be again restored, which the ordinary Course of the civil Law is unable to effect, I have thought fit to issue this my Proclamation, hereby declaring, that until the aforesaid good Purposes can be obtained, I do, in Virtue of the Power and Authority to me given, by his Majesty, determine to execute martial Law, and cause the same to be executed throughout this Colony; and to the End that Peace and good Order may the sooner be restored, I do require every Person capable of bearing Arms to resort to his Majesty's STANDARD, or be looked upon as Traitors to his Majesty's Crown and Government, and thereby become liable to the Penalty the Law inflicts upon such Offences, such as Forfeiture of Life, Confiscation of Lands, &c. &c. And I do hereby further declare all indentured Servants, Negroes, or others, (appertaining to Rebels) free, that are able and willing to bear Arms, they joining his Majesty's Troops, as soon as may be, for the more speedily reducing this Colony to a proper Sense of their Duty, to his Majesty's Crown and Dignity. I do further order, and require, all his Majesty's liege Subjects to retain their Quitrents, or any other Taxes due, or that may become due, in their own Custody, till such Time as Peace may again be restored to this at present most unhappy Country, or demanded of them for their former salutary Purposes, by Officers properly authorised to receive the same.
GIVEN under my Hand, on board the ship WILLIAM, off Norfolk, the 7th Day of November, in the 16th Year of his Majesty's Reign.
DUNMORE.
GOD SAVE THE KING

THE DELETED PASSAGE OF THE DECLARATION OF INDEPENDENCE
1776

This passage could basically be seen as a response to Dunmore's proclamation. In this removed portion of the Declaration of Independence, Thomas Jefferson writes about the horrors of enslavement and its Atlantic trade. It was met with great debate amongst the continental delegates and was removed. It was replaced with a more ambiguous grievance against the king.

He has waged cruel war against human nature itself, violating its most sacred rights of life and liberty in the persons of a distant people who never offended him, captivating & carrying them into slavery in another hemisphere or to incur miserable death in their transportation thither. This piratical warfare, the opprobrium of infidel powers, is the warfare of the Christian King of Great Britain. Determined to keep open a market where Men should be bought & sold, he has prostituted his negative for suppressing every legislative attempt to prohibit or restrain this execrable commerce. And that this assemblage of horrors might want no fact of distinguished die, he is now exciting those very people to rise in arms among us, and to purchase that liberty of which he has deprived them, by murdering the people on whom he has obtruded them: thus paying off former crimes committed again the Liberties of one people, with crimes which he urges them to commit against the lives of another.

Benjamin Banneker's Letter to Thomas Jefferson,
August 19, 1791

Banneker was a self taught mathematician and astronomer, born to free blacks in 1731.

SIR,

I AM fully sensible of the greatness of that freedom, which I take with you on the present occasion; a liberty which seemed to me scarcely allowable, when I reflected on that distinguished and dignified station in which you stand, and the almost general prejudice and prepossession, which is so prevalent in the world against those of my complexion.

I suppose it is a truth too well attested to you, to need a proof here, that we are a race of beings, who have long labored under the abuse and censure of the world; that we have long been looked upon with an eye of contempt; and that we have long been considered rather as brutish than human, and scarcely capable of mental endowments.

Sir, I hope I may safely admit, in consequence of that report which hath reached me, that you are a man far less inflexible in sentiments of this nature, than many others; that you are measurably friendly, and well disposed towards us; and that you are willing and ready to lend your aid and assistance to our relief, from those many distresses, and numerous calamities, to which we are reduced. Now Sir, if this is founded in truth, I apprehend you will embrace every opportunity, to eradicate that train of absurd and false ideas and opinions, which so generally prevails with respect to us; and that your sentiments are concurrent with mine, which are, that one universal Father hath given being to us all; and that he hath not only made us all of one flesh, but that he hath also, without partiality, afforded us all the same sensations and endowed us all with the same faculties; and that however variable we may be in society or religion, however diversified in situation or color, we are all of the same family, and stand in the same relation to him.

Sir, if these are sentiments of which you are fully persuaded, I hope you cannot but acknowledge, that it is the indispensible duty of those, who maintain for themselves the rights of human nature, and who possess the obligations of Christianity, to extend their power and influence to the relief of every part of the human race, from whatever burden or oppression they may unjustly labor under; and this, I apprehend, a full conviction of the truth and obligation of these principles should lead all to. Sir, I have long been convinced, that if your love for yourselves, and for those inestimable laws, which preserved to you the rights of human nature, was founded on sincerity, you could not but be solicitous, that every individual, of whatever rank or distinction, might with you equally enjoy the blessings thereof; neither could you rest satisfied short of the most active effusion of your exertions, in order to their promotion from any state of degradation, to which the unjustifiable cruelty and barbarism of men may have reduced them.

Sir, I freely and cheerfully acknowledge, that I am of the African race, and in that color which is natural to them of the deepest dye; and it is under a sense of the most profound gratitude to the Supreme Ruler of the Universe, that I now confess to you, that I am not under that state of tyrannical thralldom, and inhuman captivity, to which too many of my brethren are doomed, but that I have abundantly tasted of the fruition of those blessings, which proceed from that free and unequalled liberty with which you are favored; and which, I hope, you will willingly allow you have mercifully received, from the immediate hand of that Being, from whom proceedeth every good and perfect Gift.

Sir, suffer me to recal to your mind that time, in which the arms and tyranny of the British crown were exerted, with every powerful effort, in order to reduce you to a state of servitude: look back, I entreat you, on the variety of dangers to which you were exposed; reflect on that time, in which every human aid appeared unavailable, and in which even hope and fortitude wore the aspect of inability to the conflict, and you cannot but be led to a serious and grateful sense of your miraculous and providential preservation; you cannot but acknowledge, that the present freedom and tranquility which you enjoy you have mercifully received, and that it is the peculiar blessing of Heaven.

This, Sir, was a time when you cleary saw into the injustice of a state of slavery, and in which you had just apprehensions of the horrors of its condition. It was now that your abhorrence thereof was so excited, that you publicly held forth this true and invaluable doctrine, which is worthy to be recorded and remembered in all succeeding ages : "We hold these truths to be self-evident, that all men are created equal; that they are endowed by their Creator with certain unalienable rights, and that among these are, life, liberty, and the pursuit of happiness." Here was a time, in which your tender feelings for yourselves had engaged you thus to declare, you were then impressed with proper ideas of the great violation of liberty, and the free possession of those blessings, to which you were entitled by nature; but, Sir, how pitiable is it to reflect, that although you were so fully convinced of the benevolence of the Father of Mankind, and of his equal and impartial distribution of these rights and privileges, which he hath conferred upon them, that you should at the same time counteract his mercies, in detaining by fraud and violence so numerous a part of my brethren, under groaning captivity and cruel oppression, that you should at the same time be found guilty of that most criminal act, which you professedly detested in others, with respect to yourselves.

I suppose that your knowledge of the situation of my brethren, is too extensive to need a recital here; neither shall I presume to prescribe methods by which they may be relieved, otherwise than by recommending to you and all others, to wean yourselves from those narrow prejudices which you have imbibed with respect to them, and as Job proposed to his friends, "put your soul in their souls' stead;" thus shall your hearts be enlarged with kindness and benevolence towards them; and thus shall you need neither the direction of myself or others, in what manner to proceed herein. And now, Sir, although my sympathy and affection for my brethren hath caused my enlargement thus far, I ardently hope, that your candor and generosity will plead with you in my behalf, when I make known to you, that it was not originally my design; but having taken up my pen in order to direct to you, as a present, a copy of an Almanac, which I have calculated for the succeeding year, I was unexpectedly and unavoidably led thereto.

This calculation is the production of my arduous study, in this my advanced stage of life; for having long had unbounded desires to become acquainted with the secrets of nature, I have had to gratify my curiosity herein, through my own assiduous application to Astronomical Study, in which I need not recount to you the many difficulties and disadvantages, which I have had to encounter.

And although I had almost declined to make my calculation for the ensuing year, in consequence of that time which I had allotted therefor, being taken up at the Federal Territory, by the request of Mr. Andrew Ellicott, yet finding myself under several engagements to Printers of this state, to whom I had communicated my design, on my return to my place of residence, I industriously applied myself thereto, which I hope I have accomplished with correctness and accuracy; a copy of which I have taken the liberty to direct to you, and which I humbly request you will favorably receive; and although you may have the opportunity of perusing it after its publication, yet I choose to send it to you in manuscript previous thereto, that thereby you might not only have an earlier inspection, but that you might also view it in my own hand writing.

And now, Sir, I shall conclude, and subscribe myself, with the most profound respect, Your most obedient humble servant,

BENJAMIN BANNEKER

To Mr. BENJAMIN BANNEKER.
Philadelphia, August 30, 1791.

SIR,

I THANK you, sincerely, for your letter of the 19th instant, and for the Almanac it contained. No body wishes more than I do, to see such proofs as you exhibit, that nature has given to our black brethren talents equal to those of the other colors of men ; and that the appearance of the want of them, is owing merely to the degraded condition of their existence, both in Africa and America. I can add with truth, that no body wishes more ardently to see a good system commenced, for raising the condition, both of their body and mind, to what it ought to be, as far as the imbecility of their present existence, and other circumstances, which cannot be neglected, will admit.

I have taken the liberty of sending your Almanac to Monsieur de Condozett, Secretary of the Academy of Sciences at Paris, and Member of the Philanthropic Society, because I considered it as a document, to which your whole color had a right for their justification, against the doubts which have been entertained of them.

I am with great esteem, Sir, Your most obedient Humble Servant,

THOMAS JEFFERSON.

FUGITIVE SLAVE ACT
1793

This was a congressional act that helped slave owners recover escaped slaves, and imposed punishments for those that did not comply.

Chap. VII.—An Act respecting fugitives from justice, and persons escaping from the service of their masters.

Section 1. Be it enacted by the Senate and House of Representatives of the United States of America in Congress assembled, That whenever the executive authority of any state in the Union, or of either of the territories northwest or south of the river Ohio, shall demand any person as a fugitive from justice, of the executive authority of any such state or territory to which such person shall have fled, and shall moreover produce the copy of an indictment found, or an affidavit made before a magistrate of any state or territory as aforesaid, charging the person so demanded, with having committed treason, felony or other crime, certified as authentic by the governor or chief magistrate of the state or territory from whence the person so charged fled, it shall be the duty of the executive authority of the state or territory to which such person shall have fled, to cause him or her to be arrested and secured, and notice of the arrest to be given to the executive authority making such demand, or to the agent of such authority appointed to receive the fugitive, and to cause the fugitive to be delivered to such agent when he shall appear: But if no such agent shall appear within six months from the time of the arrest, the prisoner may be discharged. And all costs or expenses incurred in the apprehending, securing, and transmitting such fugitive to the state or territory making such demand, shall be paid by such state or territory.

Sec. 2. And be it further enacted, That any agent, appointed as aforesaid, who shall receive the fugitive into his custody, shall be empowered to transport him or her to the state or territory from which he or she shall have fled. And if any person or persons shall by force set at liberty, or rescue the fugitive from such agent while transporting, as aforesaid, the person or persons so offending shall, on conviction, be fined not exceeding five hundred dollars, and be imprisoned not exceeding one year.

Sec. 3. And be it also enacted, That when a person held to labour in any of the United States, or in either of the territories on the northwest or south of the river Ohio, under the laws thereof, shall escape into any other of the said states or territory, the person to whom such labour or service may be due, his agent or attorney, is hereby empowered to seize or arrest such fugitive from labour, (b) and to take him or her before any judge of the circuit or district courts of the United States, residing or being within the state, or being any magistrate of a county, city or town corporate, wherein such seizure or arrest shall be made, and upon proof to the satisfaction of such judge or magistrate, either by oral testimony or affidavit taken before and certified by a magistrate of any such state or territory, that the person so seized or arrested, doth, under the laws of the state or territory from which he or she fled, owe service or labour to the person claiming him or her, it shall be the duty of such judge or magistrate to give a certificate thereof to such claimant, his agent or attorney, which shall be sufficient warrant for removing the said fugitive from labour, to the state or territory from which he or she fled.

39

Sec. 4. And be it further enacted, That any person who shall knowingly and willingly obstruct or hinder such claimant, his agent or attorney in so seizing or arresting such fugitive from labour, or shall rescue such fugitive from such claimant, his agent or attorney when so arrested pursuant to the authority herein given or declared; or shall harbor or conceal such person after notice that he or she was a fugitive from labour, as aforesaid, shall for either of the said offences, forfeit and pay the sum of five hundred dollars. Which penalty may be recovered by and for the benefit of such claimant, by the action of debt, in any court proper to try the same; saving moreover to the person claiming such labour or service, his right of action for or on account of the said injuries or either of them.

Approved, February 12, 1793

UNITED STATES V. THE AMISTAD
1841

A slave rebellion on a ship bound for Cuban plantations led to a Supreme Court case that found in favor of the slaves aboard. They gained their freedom, with many returning to Africa thanks to funding by the United Missionary Society.

Decided March 9, 1841

MR. JUSTICE STORY delivered the opinion of the Court.

This is the case of an appeal from the decree of the Circuit Court of the District of Connecticut, sitting in admiralty. The leading facts, as they appear upon the transcript of the proceedings, are as follows: On the 27th of June, 1839, the schooner L'Amistad, being the property of Spanish subjects, cleared out from the port of Havana, in the island of Cuba, for Puerto Principe, in the same island. On board of the schooner were the captain, Ransom Ferrer, and Jose Ruiz, and Pedro Montez, all Spanish subjects. The former had with him a negro boy, named Antonio, claimed to be his slave. Jose Ruiz had with him forty-nine negroes, claimed by him as his slaves, and stated to be his property, in a certain pass or document, signed by the Governor General of Cuba. Pedro Montez had with him four other negroes, also claimed by him as his slaves, and stated to be his property, in a similar pass or document, also signed by the Governor General [*588] of Cuba. On the voyage, and before the arrival of the vessel at her port of destination, the negroes rose, killed the captain, and took possession of her. On the 26th of August, the vessel was discovered by Lieutenant Gedney, of the United States brig Washington, at anchor on the high seas, at the distance of half a mile from the shore of Long Island. A part of the negroes were then on shore at Culloden Point, Long Island; who were seized by Lieutenant Gedney, and brought on board. The vessel, with the negroes and other persons on board, was brought by Lieutenant Gedney into the district of Connecticut, and there libeled for salvage in the District Court of the United States. A libel for salvage was also filed by Henry Green and Pelatiah Fordham, of Sag Harbour, Long Island. On the 18th of September, Ruiz and Montez filed claims and libels, in which they asserted their ownership of the negroes as their slaves, and of certain parts of the cargo, and prayed that the same might be "delivered to them, or to the representatives of her Catholic majesty, as might be most proper." On the 19th of September, the Attorney of the United states, for the district of Connecticut, filed an information or libel, setting forth, that the Spanish minister had officially presented to the proper department of the government of the United States, a claim for the restoration of the vessel, cargo, and slaves, as the property of Spanish subjects, which had arrived within the jurisdictional limits of the United States, and were taken possession of by the said public armed brig of the United States; under such circumstances as made it the duty of the United States to cause the same to be restored to the true proprietors, pursuant to the treaty between the United States and Spain: and praying the Court, on its being made legally to appear that the claim of the Spanish minister was well founded, to make such order for the disposal of the vessel, cargo, and slaves, as would best enable the United States to comply with their treaty stipulations. But if it should appear, that the negroes were persons transported from Africa, in violation of the laws of the United States, and brought within the United States contrary to the same laws; he then prayed the Court to make such order for their removal to the coast of Africa, pursuant to the laws of the United States, as it should deem fit.

On the 19th of November, the Attorney of the United States filed a second information or libel, similar to the first, with the exception of the second prayer above set forth in his former one. On the same day, Antonio G. Vega, the vice-consul of Spain, for the state of Connecticut, filed his libel, alleging that Antonio was a slave, the property of the representatives of Ramon Ferrer, and praying the Court to cause him to be delivered to the said vice-consul, that he might be returned by him to his lawful owner in the island of Cuba.

On the 7th of January, 1840, the negroes, Cinque and others, with the exception of Antonio, by their counsel, filed an answer, denying that they were slaves, or the property of Ruiz and Montez, or that the Court could, under the Constitution or laws of the United States, or under any treaty, exercise any jurisdiction over their persons, by reason of the premises; and praying that they might be dismissed. They specially set forth and insist in this answer, that they were native born Africans; born free, and still of right ought to be free and not slaves; that they were, on or about the 15th of April, 1839, unlawfully kidnapped, and forcibly and wrongfully carried on board a certain vessel on the coast of Africa, which was unlawfully engaged in the slave trade, and were unlawfully transported in the same vessel to the island of Cuba, for the purpose of being there unlawfully sold as slaves; that Ruiz and Montez, well knowing the premises, made a pretended purchase of them: that afterwards, on or about the 28th of June, 1839, Ruiz and Montez, confederating with Ferrer, (captain of the Amistad,) caused them, without law or right, to be placed on board of the Amistad, to be transported to some place unknown to them, and there to be enslaved for life; that, on the voyage, they rose on the master, and took possession of the vessel, intending to return therewith to their native country, or to seek an asylum in some free state; and the vessel arrived, about the 26th of August, 1839, off Montauk Point, near Long Island; a part of them were sent on shore, and were seized by Lieutenant Gedney, and carried on board; and all of them were afterwards brought by him into the district of Connecticut.

On the 7th of January, 1840, Jose Antonio Tellincas, and Messrs. Aspe and Laca, all Spanish subjects, residing in Cuba, filed their claims, as owners to certain portions of the goods found on board of the schooner L'Amistad.

On the same day, all the libellants and claimants, by their counsel, except Jose Ruiz and Pedro Montez, (whose libels and claims, as stated of record, respectively, were pursued by the Spanish minister, the same being merged in his claims,) appeared, and the negroes also appeared by their counsel; and the case was heard on the libels, claims, answers, and testimony of witnesses.

On the 23d day of January, 1840, the District Court made a decree. By that decree, the Court rejected the claim of Green and Fordham for salvage, but allowed salvage to Lieutenant Gedney and others, on the vessel and cargo, of one-third of the value thereof, but not on the negroes, Cinque and others; it allowed the claim of Tellincas, and Aspe and Laca with the exception of the above-mentioned salvage; it dismissed the libels and claims of Ruiz and Montez, with costs, as being included under the claim of the Spanish minister; it allowed the claim of the Spanish vice-consul for Antonio, on behalf of Ferrer's representatives; it rejected the claims of Ruiz and Montez for the delivery of the negroes, but admitted them for the cargo, with the exception of the above-mentioned salvage; it rejected the claim made by the Attorney of the United States on behalf of the Spanish minister, for the restoration of the negroes under the treaty; but it decreed that they should be delivered to the President of the United States, to be transported to Africa, pursuant to the act of 3d March, 1819.

From this decree the District Attorney, on behalf of the United States, appealed to the Circuit Court, except so far as related to the restoration of the slave Antonio. The claimants, Tellincas, and Aspe and Laca, also appealed from that part of the decree which awarded salvage on the property respectively claimed by them. No appeal was interposed by Ruiz or Montez, or on behalf of the representatives of the owners of the Amistad. The Circuit Court, by a mere pro forma decree, affirmed the decree of the District Court, reserving the question of salvage upon the claims of Tellincas, and Aspe and Laca. And from that decree the present appeal has been brought to this Court.

The cause has been very elaborately argued, as well upon the merits, as upon a motion on behalf of the appellees to dismiss the appeal. On the part of the United States, it has been contended, 1. That due and sufficient proof concerning the property has been made to authorize the restitution of the vessel, cargo, and negroes to the Spanish subjects on whose behalf they are claimed pursuant to the treaty with Spain, of the 27th of October, 1795. 2. That the United States had a right to intervene in the manner in which they have done, to obtain a decree for the restitution of the property, upon the application of the Spanish minister. These propositions have been strenuously denied on the other side. Other collateral and incidental points have been stated, upon which it is not necessary at this moment to dwell.

Before entering upon the discussion of the main points involved in this interesting and important controversy, it may be necessary to say a few words as to the actual posture of the case as it now stands before us. In the first place, then, the only parties now before the Court on one side, are the United States, intervening for the sole purpose of procuring restitution of the property as Spanish property, pursuant to the treaty, upon the grounds stated by the other parties claiming the property in their respective libels. The United States do not assert any property in themselves, or any violation of their own rights, or sovereignty, or laws, by the acts complained of. They do not insist that these negroes have been imported into the United States, in contravention of our own slave trade acts. They do not seek to have these negroes delivered up for the purpose of being transported to Cuba as pirates or robbers, or as fugitive criminals against the laws of Spain. They do not assert that the seizure, and bringing the vessel, and cargo, and negroes into port, by Lieutenant Gedney, for the purpose of adjudication, is a tortious act. They simply confine themselves to the right of the Spanish claimants to the restitution of their property, upon the facts asserted in their respective allegations.

In the next place, the parties before the Court on the other side as appellees, are Lieutenant Gedney, on his libel for salvage, and the negroes, (Cinque, and others,) asserting themselves, in their answer, not to be slaves, but free native Africans, kidnapped in their own country, and illegally transported by force from that country; and now entitled to maintain their freedom.

No question has been here made, as to the proprietary interests in the vessel and cargo. It is admitted that they belong to Spanish subjects, and that they ought to be restored. The only point on this head is, whether the restitution ought to be upon the payment of salvage or not? The main controversy is, whether these negroes are the property of Ruiz and Montez, and ought to be delivered up; and to this, accordingly, we shall first direct our attention.

It has been argued on behalf of the United States, that the Court are bound to deliver them up, according to the treaty of 1795, with Spain, which has in this particular been continued in full force, by the treaty of 1819, ratified in 1821. The sixth article of that treaty, seems to have had, principally, in view cases where the property of the subjects of either state had been taken possession of within the territorial jurisdiction of the other, during war. The eighth article provides for cases where the shipping of the inhabitants of either state are forced, through stress of weather, pursuit of pirates, or enemies, or any other urgent necessity, to seek shelter in the ports of the other. There may well be some doubt entertained, whether the present case, in its actual circumstances, falls within the purview of this article. But it does not seem necessary, for reasons hereafter stated, absolutely to decide it. The ninth article provides, "that all ships and merchandise, of what nature soever, which shall be rescued out of the hands of any pirates or robbers, on the high seas, shall be brought into some port of either state, and shall be delivered to the custody of the officers of that port, in order to be taken care of and restored entire to the true proprietor, as soon as due and sufficient proof shall be made concerning the property thereof." This is the article on which the main reliance is placed on behalf of the United States, for the restitution of these negroes. To bring the case within the article, it is essential to establish, First, That these negroes, under all the circumstances, fall within the description of merchandise, in the sense of the treaty. Secondly, That there has been a rescue of them on the high seas, out of the hands of the pirates and robbers; which, in the present case, can only be, by showing that they themselves are pirates and robbers; and, Thirdly, That Ruiz and Montez, the asserted proprietors, are the true proprietors, and have established their title by competent proof.

If these negroes were, at the time, lawfully held as slaves under the laws of Spain, and recognised by those laws as property capable of being lawfully bought and sold; we see no reason why they may not justly be deemed within the intent of the treaty, to be included under the denomination of merchandise, and, as such, ought to be restored to the claimants: for, upon that point, the laws of Spain would seem to furnish the proper rule of interpretation. But, admitting this, it is clear, in our opinion, that neither of the other essential facts and requisites has been established in proof; and the onus probandi of both lies upon the claimants to give rise to the causes foederis. It is plain beyond controversy, if we examine the evidence, that these negroes never were the lawful slaves of Ruiz or Montez, or of any other Spanish subjects. They are natives of Africa, and were kidnapped there, and were unlawfully transported to Cuba, in violation of the laws and treaties of Spain, and the most solemn edicts and declarations of that government. By those laws, and treaties, and edicts, the African slave trade is utterly abolished; the dealing in that trade is deemed a heinous crime; and the negroes thereby introduced into the dominions of Spain, are declared to be free. Ruiz and Montez are proved to have made the pretended purchase of these negroes, with a full knowledge of all the circumstances. And so cogent and irresistible is the evidence in this respect, that the District Attorney has admitted in open Court, upon the record, that these negroes were native Africans, and recently imported into Cuba, as alleged in their answers to the libels in the case. The supposed proprietary interest of Ruiz and Montez, is completely displaced, if we are at liberty to look at the evidence of the admissions of the District Attorney.

If, then, these negroes are not slaves, but are kidnapped Africans, who, by the laws of Spain itself, are entitled to their freedom, and were kidnapped and illegally carried to Cuba, and illegally detained and restrained on board of the Amistad; there is no pretence to say, that they are pirates or robbers. We may lament the dreadful acts, by which they asserted their liberty, and took possession of the Amistad, and endeavoured to regain their native country; but they cannot be deemed pirates or robbers in the sense of the law of nations, or the treaty with Spain, or the laws of Spain itself; at least so far as those laws have been brought to our knowledge. Nor do the libels of Ruiz or Montez assert them to be such.

This posture of the facts would seem, of itself, to put an end to the Whole inquiry upon the merits. But it is argued, on behalf of the United States, that the ship, and cargo, and negroes were duly documented as belonging to Spanish subjects, and this Court have no right to look behind these documents; that full faith and credit is to be given to them; and that they are to be held conclusive evidence in this cause, even although it should be established by the most satisfactory proofs, that they have been obtained by the grossest frauds and impositions upon the constituted authorities of Spain. To this argument we can, in no wise, assent. There is nothing in the treaty which justifies or sustains the argument. We do not here meddle with the point, whether there has been any connivance in this illegal traffic, on the part of any of the colonial authorities or subordinate officers of Cuba; because, in our view, such an examination is unnecessary, and ought not to be pursued, unless it were indispensable to public justice, although it has been strongly pressed at the bar. What we proceed upon is this, that although public documents of the government, accompanying property found on board of the private ships of a foreign nation, certainly are to be deemed prima facie evidence of the facts which they purport to state, yet they are always open to be impugned for fraud; and whether that fraud be in the original obtaining of these documents, or in the subsequent fraudulent and illegal use of them, when once it is satisfactorily established, it overthrows all their sanctity, and destroys them as proof. Fraud will vitiate any, even the most solemn transactions; and an asserted title to property, founded upon it, is utterly void. The very language of the ninth article of the treaty of 1795, requires the proprietor to make due and sufficient proof of his property. And how can that proof be deemed either due or sufficient, which is but a connected, and stained tissue of fraud? This is not a mere rule of municipal jurisprudence. Nothing is more clear in the law of nations, as an established rule to regulate their rights, and duties, and intercourse, than the doctrine, that the ship's papers are but prima facie evidence, and that, if they are shown to be fraudulent, they are not to be held proof of any valid title. This rule is familiarly applied, and, indeed, is of every-days occurrence in cases of prize, in the contests between belligerents and neutrals, as is apparent from numerous cases to be found in the Reports of this Court; and it is just as applicable to the transactions of civil intercourse between nations in times of peace. If a private ship, clothed with Spanish papers, should enter the ports of the United States, claiming the privileges, and immunities, and rights belonging to bona fide subjects of Spain, under our treaties or laws, and she should, in reality, belong to the subjects of another nation, which was not entitled to any such privileges, immunities, or rights, and the proprietors were seeking, by fraud, to cover their own illegal acts, under the flag of Spain; there can be no doubt, that it would be the duty of our Courts to strip off the disguise, and to look at the case according to its naked realities. In the solemn treaties between nations, it can never be presumed that either state intends to provide the means of perpetrating or protecting frauds; but all the provisions are to be construed as intended to be applied to bona fide transactions. The seventeenth article of the treaty with Spain, which provides for certain passports and certificates, as evidence of property on board of the ships of both states, is, in its terms, applicable only to cases where either of the parties is engaged in a war. This article required a certain form of passport to be agreed upon by the parties, and annexed to the treaty. It never was annexed; and, therefore, in the case of the Amiable Isabella, 6 Wheaton, 1, it was held inoperative.

It is also a most important consideration in the present case, which ought not to be lost sight of, that, supposing these African negroes not to be slaves, but kidnapped, and free negroes, the treaty with Spain cannot be obligatory upon them; and the United States are bound to respect their rights as much as those of Spanish subjects. The conflict of rights between the parties under such circumstances, becomes positive and inevitable, and must be decided upon the eternal principles of justice and international law. If the contest were about any goods on board of this ship, to which American citizens asserted a title, which was denied by the Spanish claimants, there could be no doubt of the right of such American citizens to litigate their claims before any competent American tribunal, notwithstanding the treaty with Spain. A fortiori, the doctrine must apply where human life and human liberty are in issue; and constitute the very essence of the controversy. The treaty with Spain never could have intended to take away the equal rights of all foreigners, who should contest their claims before any of our Courts, to equal justice; or to deprive such foreigners of the protection given them by other treaties, or by the general law of nations. Upon the merits of the case, then, there does not seem to us to be any ground for doubt, that these negroes ought to be deemed free; and that the Spanish treaty interposes no obstacle to the just assertion of their rights.

There is another consideration growing out of this part of the case, which necessarily rises in judgment. It is observable, that the United States, in their original claim, filed it in the alternative, to have the negroes, if slaves and Spanish property, restored to the proprietors; or, if not slaves, but negroes who had been transported from Africa, in violation of the laws of the United States, and brought into the United States contrary to the same laws, then the Court to pass an order to enable the United States to remove such persons to the coast of Africa, to be delivered there to such agent as may be authorized to receive and provide for them. At a subsequent period, this last alternative claim was not insisted on, and another claim was interposed, omitting it; from which the conclusion naturally arises that it was abandoned. The decree of the District Court, however, contained an order for the delivery of the negroes to the United States, to be transported to the coast of Africa, under the act of the 3d of March, 1819, ch. 224. The United States do not now insist upon any affirmance of this part of the decree; and, in our judgment, upon the admitted facts, there is no ground to assert that the case comes within the purview of the act of 1819, or of any other of our prohibitory slave trade acts. These negroes were never taken from Africa, or brought to the United States in contravention of those acts. When the Amistad arrived she was in possession of the negroes, asserting their freedom; and in no sense could they possibly intend to import themselves here, as [*597] slaves, or for sale as slaves. In this view of the matter, that part of the decree of the District Court is unmaintainable, and must be reversed.

The view which has been thus taken of this case, upon the merits, under the first point, renders it wholly unnecessary for us to give any opinion upon the other point, as to the right of the United States to intervene in this case in the manner already stated. We dismiss this, therefore, as well as several minor points made at the argument.

As to the claim of Lieutenant Gedney for the salvage service, it is understood that the United States do not now desire to interpose any obstacle to the allowance of it, if it is deemed reasonable by the Court. It was a highly meritorious and useful service to the proprietors of the ship and cargo; and such as, by the general principles of maritime law, is always deemed a just foundation for salvage. The rate allowed by the Court, does not seem to us to have been beyond the exercise of a sound discretion, under the very peculiar and embarrassing circumstances of the case.

Upon the whole, our opinion is, that the decree of the Circuit Court, affirming that of the District Court, ought to be affirmed, except so far as it directs the negroes to be delivered to the President, to be transported to Africa, in pursuance of the act of the 3d of March, 1819; and, as to this, it ought to be reversed: and that the said negroes be declared to be free, and be dismissed from the custody of the Court, and go without day.

DISSENT: MR. JUSTICE BALDWIN dissented.

This cause came on to be heard on the transcript of the record from the Circuit Court of the United States, for the District of Connecticut, and was argued by counsel. On consideration whereof, it is the opinion of this Court, that there is error in that part of the decree of the Circuit Court, affirming the decree of the District Court, which ordered the said negroes to be delivered to the President of the United States, to be transported to Africa, in pursuance of the act of Congress, of the 3d of March, 1819; and that, as to that part, it ought to be reversed: and, in all other respects, that the said decree of the [*598] Circuit Court ought to be affirmed. It is therefore ordered adjudged, and decreed by this Court, that the decree of the said Circuit Court be, and the same is hereby, affirmed, except as to the part aforesaid, and as to that part, that it be reversed; and that the cause be remanded to the Circuit Court, with directions to enter, in lieu of that part, a decree, that the said negroes be, and are hereby, declared to be free, and that they be dismissed from the custody of the Court, and be discharged from the suit and go thereof quit without day.

OREGON EXCLUSION LAWS 1849-1857

These were a series of laws set to prohibit slavery in the Oregon territory and later the state. It also prohibited all blacks from the territory as well. Lashings would be given for those blacks that refused to leave the state.

Sect. 1 Be it enacted by the Legislative Assembly of the Territory of Oregon that it shall not be lawful for any negro or mulatto to enter into, or reside within the limits of this Territory. Providing that nothing in this act shall ....apply to any negro or mulatto now resident in this Territory, nor shall it apply to the offspring of any such as are resi¬dents....

Sect. 2 That Masters and owners of vessels having negroes or mulattoes in their employ on board of vessel may bring them into Oregon Provided that in so doing such master, or owner, shall be responsible for the conduct of such negro or mulatto....and shall be liable to any person aggrieved by such negro or mulatto.

Sect. 3 No negro or mulatto shall be permitted to leave the port where the vessel upon which they are or may be employed shall be lying without the written permission of such master or owner....

Sect. 4 That it shall be the duty of masters and owners of vessels having brought negroes or mulattoes into Oregon as aforesaid to cause such negro or mulatto to leave this territory with such vessel upon which the shall have been brought into the Territory, or from some other vessel within forty days.

Sect. 5 If any master or owners of a vessel having brought negroes or mulattoes as provided for in the second section of this act into this Territory, shall fail to remove and take the same with them when leaving the Territory.... shall be deemed guilty of a misdemeanor....and on conviction, shall be fined and imprisoned at the discretion of the court; Provided that the fine in no case shall be less than five hundred dollars.

Sect. 6 If any negro or mulatto shall be found in this Territory, except as hereinbefore provided and except such as may now be permanent residents, it shall be the duty of any Judge or Justice of the Peace to....to issue a warrant for the apprehension of such negro or mulatto, directed to any sheriff or constable....to arrest....such negro or mulat¬to....

Sect. 7 If any negro or mulatto shall be found a second time unlawfully remaining in this Territory he shall be deemed guilty of a misdemeanor and shall....upon conviction be fined and imprisoned at the discretion of the court.

Sect. 8 The Governor of this Territory shall cause this act to be published in some one or more of the California newspapers and such other newspapers as he may think necessary in order to carry out the spirit of the same.

Sect. 9 This act to take effect and be in force from and after its passage.

FUGITIVE SLAVE ACT
1850

This version of the Fugitive Slave Act gave more severe penalties for those slaves that escaped and for those hindering their capture.

Approved, September 18, 1850

Be it enacted by the Senate and House of Representatives of the United States of America in Congress assembled, That the persons who have been, or may hereafter be, appointed commissioners, in virtue of any act of Congress, by the Circuit Courts of the United States, and Who, in consequence of such appointment, are authorized to exercise the powers that any justice of the peace, or other magistrate of any of the United States, may exercise in respect to offenders for any crime or offense against the United States, by arresting, imprisoning, or bailing the same under and by the virtue of the thirty-third section of the act of the twenty-fourth of September seventeen hundred and eighty-nine, entitled "An Act to establish the judicial courts of the United States" shall be, and are hereby, authorized and required to exercise and discharge all the powers and duties conferred by this act.

Sec. 2.
And be it further enacted, That the Superior Court of each organized Territory of the United States shall have the same power to appoint commissioners to take acknowledgments of bail and affidavits, and to take depositions of witnesses in civil causes, which is now possessed by the Circuit Court of the United States; and all commissioners who shall hereafter be appointed for such purposes by the Superior Court of any organized Territory of the United States, shall possess all the powers, and exercise all the duties, conferred by law upon the commissioners appointed by the Circuit Courts of the United States for similar purposes, and shall moreover exercise and discharge all the powers and duties conferred by this act.

Sec. 3.
And be it further enacted, That the Circuit Courts of the United States shall from time to time enlarge the number of the commissioners, with a view to afford reasonable facilities to reclaim fugitives from labor, and to the prompt discharge of the duties imposed by this act.

Sec. 4.
And be it further enacted, That the commissioners above named shall have concurrent jurisdiction with the judges of the Circuit and District Courts of the United States, in their respective circuits and districts within the several States, and the judges of the Superior Courts of the Territories, severally and collectively, in term-time and vacation; shall grant certificates to such claimants, upon satisfactory proof being made, with authority to ake and remove such fugitives from service or labor, under the restrictions herein contained, to the State or Territory from which such persons may have escaped or fled.

Sec. 5.

And be it further enacted, That it shall be the duty of all marshals and deputy marshals to obey and execute all warrants and precepts issued under the provisions of this act, when to them directed; and should any marshal or deputy marshal refuse to receive such warrant, or other process, when tendered, or to use all proper means diligently to execute the same, he shall, on conviction thereof, be fined in the sum of one thousand dollars, to the use of such claimant, on the motion of such claimant, by the Circuit or District Court for the district of such marshal; and after arrest of such fugitive, by such marshal or his deputy, or whilst at any time in his custody under the provisions of this act, should such fugitive escape, whether with or without the assent of such marshal or his deputy, such marshal shall be liable, on his official bond, to be prosecuted for the benefit of such claimant, for the full value of the service or labor of said fugitive in the State, Territory, or District whence he escaped: and the better to enable the said commissioners, when thus appointed, to execute their duties faithfully and efficiently, in conformity with the requirements of the Constitution of the United States and of this act, they are hereby authorized and empowered, within their counties respectively, to appoint, in writing under their hands, any one or more suitable persons, from time to time, to execute all such warrants and other process as may be issued by them in the lawful performance of their respective duties; with authority to such commissioners, or the persons to be appointed by them, to execute process as aforesaid, to summon and call to their aid the bystanders, or posse comitatus of the proper county, when necessary to ensure a faithful observance of the clause of the Constitution referred to, in conformity with the provisions of this act; and all good citizens are hereby commanded to aid and assist in the prompt and efficient execution of this law, whenever their services may be required, as aforesaid, for that purpose; and said warrants shall run, and be executed by said officers, anywhere in the State within which they are issued.

Sec. 6.

And be it further enacted, That when a person held to service or labor in any State or Territory of the United States, ha: heretofore or shall hereafter escape into another State or Territory of the United States, the person or persons to whom such service 01 labor may be due, or his, her, or their agent or attorney, duly authorized, by power of attorney, in writing, acknowledged and certified under the seal of some legal officer or court of the State or Territory in which the same may be executed, may pursue and reclaim such fugitive person, either by procuring a warrant from some one of the courts, judges, or commissioners aforesaid, of the proper circuit, district, or county, for the apprehension of such fugitive from service or labor, or by seizing and arresting such fugitive, where the same can be done without process, and by taking, or causing such person to be taken, forthwith before such court, judge, or commissioner, whose duty it shall be to hear and determine the case of such claimant in a summary manner; and upon satisfactory proof being made, by deposition or affidavit, in writing, to be taken and certified by such court, judge, or commissioner, or by other satisfactory testimony, duly taken and certified by some court, magistrate, justice of the peace, or other legal officer authorized to administer an oath and take depositions under the laws of the State or Territory from which such person owing service or labor may have escaped, with a certificate of such magistracy or other authority, as aforesaid, with the seal of the proper court or officer thereto attached, which seal shall be sufficient to establish the competency of the proof, and with proof, also by affidavit, of the identity of the person whose service or labor is claimed to be due as aforesaid, that the person so arrested does in fact owe service or labor to the person or persons claiming him or her, in the State or Territory from which such fugitive may have escaped as aforesaid, and that said person escaped, to make out and deliver to such claimant, his or her agent or attorney, a certificate setting forth the substantial facts as to the service or labor due from such fugitive to the claimant, and of his or her escape from the State or Territory in which he or she was arrested, with authority to such claimant, or his or her agent or attorney, to use such reasonable force and restraint as may be necessary, under the circumstances of the case, to take and remove such fugitive person back to the State or Territory whence he or she may have escaped as aforesaid. In no trial or hearing under this act shall the testimony of such alleged fugitive be admitted in evidence; and the certificates in this and the first [fourth] section mentioned, shall be conclusive of the right of the person or persons in whose favor granted, to remove such fugitive to the State or Territory from which he escaped, and shall prevent all molestation of such person or persons by any process issued by any court, judge, magistrate, or other person whomsoever.

Sec. 7.

And be it further enacted, That any person who shall knowingly and willingly obstruct, hinder, or prevent such claimant, his agent or attorney, or any person or persons lawfully assisting him, her, or them, from arresting such a fugitive from service or labor, either with or without process as aforesaid, or shall rescue, or attempt to rescue, such fugitive from service or labor, from the custody of such claimant, his or her agent or attorney, or other person or persons lawfully assisting as aforesaid, when so arrested, pursuant to the authority herein given and declared; or shall aid, abet, or assist such person so owing service or labor as aforesaid, directly or indirectly, to escape from such claimant, his agent or attorney, or other person or persons legally authorized as aforesaid; or shall harbor or conceal such fugitive, so as to prevent the discovery and arrest of such person, after notice or knowledge of the fact that such person was a fugitive from service or labor as aforesaid, shall, for either of said offences, be subject to a fine not exceeding one thousand dollars, and imprisonment not exceeding six months, by indictment and conviction before the District Court of the United States for the district in which such offence may have been committed, or before the proper court of criminal jurisdiction, if committed within any one of the organized Territories of the United States; and shall moreover forfeit and pay, by way of civil damages to the party injured by such illegal conduct, the sum of one thousand dollars for each fugitive so lost as aforesaid, to be recovered by action of debt, in any of the District or Territorial Courts aforesaid, within whose jurisdiction the said offence may have been committed.

Sec. 8.
And be it further enacted, That the marshals, their deputies, and the clerks of the said District and Territorial Courts, shall be paid, for their services, the like fees as may be allowed for similar services in other cases; and where such services are rendered exclusively in the arrest, custody, and delivery of the fugitive to the claimant, his or her agent or attorney, or where such supposed fugitive may be discharged out of custody for the want of sufficient proof as aforesaid, then such fees are to be paid in whole by such claimant, his or her agent or attorney; and in all cases where the proceedings are before a commissioner, he shall be entitled to a fee of ten dollars in full for his services in each case, upon the delivery of the said certificate to the claimant, his agent or attorney; or a fee of five dollars in cases where the proof shall not, in the opinion of such commissioner, warrant such certificate and delivery, inclusive of all services incident to such arrest and examination, to be paid, in either case, by the claimant, his or her agent or attorney. The person or persons authorized to execute the process to be issued by such commissioner for the arrest and detention of fugitives from service or labor as aforesaid, shall also be entitled to a fee of five dollars each for each person he or they may arrest, and take before any commissioner as aforesaid, at the instance and request of such claimant, with such other fees as may be deemed reasonable by such commissioner for such other additional services as may be necessarily performed by him or them; such as attending at the examination, keeping the fugitive in custody, and providing him with food and lodging during his detention, and until the final determination of such commissioners; and, in general, for performing such other duties as may be required by such claimant, his or her attorney or agent, or commissioner in the premises, such fees to be made up in conformity with the fees usually charged by the officers of the courts of justice within the proper district or county, as near as may be practicable, and paid by such claimants, their agents or attorneys, whether such supposed fugitives from service or labor be ordered to be delivered to such claimant by the final determination of such commissioner or not.

Sec. 9.

And be it further enacted, That, upon affidavit made by the claimant of such fugitive, his agent or attorney, after such certificate has been issued, that he has reason to apprehend that such fugitive will be rescued by force from his or their possession before he can be taken beyond the limits of the State in which the arrest is made, it shall be the duty of the officer making the arrest to retain such fugitive in his custody, and to remove him to the State whence he fled, and there to deliver him to said claimant, his agent, or attorney. And to this end, the officer aforesaid is hereby authorized and required to employ so many persons as he may deem necessary to overcome such force, and to retain them in his service so long as circumstances may require. The said officer and his assistants, while so employed, to receive the same compensation, and to be allowed the same expenses, as are now allowed by law for transportation of criminals, to be certified by the judge of the district within which the arrest is made, and paid out of the treasury of the United States.

Sec. 10.

And be it further enacted, That when any person held to service or labor in any State or Territory, or in the District of Columbia, shall escape therefrom, the party to whom such service or labor shall be due, his, her, or their agent or attorney, may apply to any court of record therein, or judge thereof in vacation, and make satisfactory proof to such court, or judge in vacation, of the escape aforesaid, and that the person escaping owed service or labor to such party. Whereupon the court shall cause a record to be made of the matters so proved, and also a general description of the person so escaping, with such convenient certainty as may be; and a transcript of such record, authenticated by the attestation of the clerk and of the seal of the said court, being produced in any other State, Territory, or district in which the person so escaping may be found, and being exhibited to any judge, commissioner, or other officer authorized by the law of the United States to cause persons escaping from service or labor to be delivered up, shall be held and taken to be full and conclusive evidence of the fact of escape, and that the service or labor of the person escaping is due to the party in such record mentioned. And upon the production by the said party of other and further evidence if necessary, either oral or by affidavit, in addition to what is contained in the said record of the identity of the person escaping, he or she shall be delivered up to the claimant. And the said court, commissioner, judge, or other person authorized by this act to grant certificates to claimants or fugitives, shall, upon the production of the record and other evidences aforesaid, grant to such claimant a certificate of his right to take any such person identified and proved to be owing service or labor as aforesaid, which certificate shall authorize such claimant to seize or arrest and transport such person to the State or Territory from which he escaped: Provided, That nothing herein contained shall be construed as requiring the production of a transcript of such record as evidence as aforesaid. But in its absence the claim shall be heard and determined upon other satisfactory proofs, competent in law.

Sojourner Truth: Ain't I A Woman?
1851
Women's Convention, Ohio

Truth was a women's rights advocate and early abolitionist. She was born into slavery as Isabella Baumfree in 1797. She changed her name decades later, believing it was God's will for her to escape slavery. .

Well, children, where there is so much racket there must be something out of kilter. I think that 'twixt the negroes of the South and the women at the North, all talking about rights, the white men will be in a fix pretty soon. But what's all this here talking about?

That man over there says that women need to be helped into carriages, and lifted over ditches, and to have the best place everywhere. Nobody ever helps me into carriages, or over mud-puddles, or gives me any best place! And ain't I a woman? Look at me! Look at my arm! I have ploughed and planted, and gathered into barns, and no man could head me! And ain't I a woman? I could work as much and eat as much as a man - when I could get it - and bear the lash as well! And ain't I a woman? I have borne thirteen children, and seen most all sold off to slavery, and when I cried out with my mother's grief, none but Jesus heard me! And ain't I a woman?

Then they talk about this thing in the head; what's this they call it? [member of audience whispers, "intellect"] That's it, honey. What's that got to do with women's rights or negroes' rights? If my cup won't hold but a pint, and yours holds a quart, wouldn't you be mean not to let me have my little half measure full?

Then that little man in black there, he says women can't have as much rights as men, 'cause Christ wasn't a woman! Where did your Christ come from? Where did your Christ come from? From God and a woman! Man had nothing to do with Him.

If the first woman God ever made was strong enough to turn the world upside down all alone, these women together ought to be able to turn it back , and get it right side up again! And now they is asking to do it, the men better let them.

Obliged to you for hearing me, and now old Sojourner ain't got nothing more to say.

Frederick Douglass Fourth of July Speech
1852

Douglass discusses the hypocrisy of freedom and justice and the values that the United States stands for, when slavery exists. Those in bondage were never able to taste the values that were fought for during the American Revolution.

Mr. President, Friends and Fellow Citizens: He who could address this audience without a quailing sensation, has stronger nerves than I have. I do not remember ever to have appeared as a speaker before any assembly more shrinkingly, nor with greater distrust of my ability, than I do this day. A feeling has crept over me, quite unfavorable to the exercise of my limited powers of speech. The task before me is one which requires much previous thought and study for its proper performance. I know that apologies of this sort are generally considered flat and unmeaning. I trust, however, that mine will not be so considered. Should I seem at ease, my appearance would much misrepresent me. The little experience I have had in addressing public meetings, in country schoolhouses, avails me nothing on the present occasion.

The papers and placards say, that I am to deliver a 4th [of] July oration. This certainly sounds large, and out of the common way, for it is true that I have often had the privilege to speak in this beautiful Hall, and to address many who now honor me with their presence. But neither their familiar faces, nor the perfect gage I think I have of Corinthian Hall, seems to free me from embarrassment.

The fact is, ladies and gentlemen, the distance between this platform and the slave plantation, from which I escaped, is considerable—and the difficulties to be overcome in getting from the latter to the former, are by no means slight. That I am here today is, to me, a matter of astonishment as well as of gratitude. You will not, therefore, be surprised, if in what I have to say, I evince no elaborate preparation, nor grace my speech with any high sounding exordium. With little experience and with less learning, I have been able to throw my thoughts hastily and imperfectly together; and trusting to your patient and generous indulgence, I will proceed to lay them before you.

This, for the purpose of this celebration, is the 4th of July. It is the birthday of your National Independence, and of your political freedom. This, to you, is what the Passover was to the emancipated people of God. It carries your minds back to the day, and to the act of your great deliverance; and to the signs, and to the wonders, associated with that act, and that day. This celebration also marks the beginning of another year of your national life; and reminds you that the Republic of America is now 76 years old. I am glad, fellow-citizens, that your nation is so young. Seventy-six years, though a good old age for a man, is but a mere speck in the life of a nation. Three score years and ten is the allotted time for individual men; but nations number their years by thousands. According to this fact, you are, even now, only in the beginning of your national career, still lingering in the period of childhood. I repeat, I am glad this is so. There is hope in the thought, and hope is much needed, under the dark clouds which lower above the horizon. The eye of the reformer is met with angry flashes, portending disastrous times; but his heart may well beat lighter at the thought that America is young, and that she is still in the impressionable stage of her existence. May he not hope that high lessons of wisdom, of justice and of truth, will yet give direction to her destiny? Were the nation older, the patriot's heart might be sadder, and the reformer's brow heavier. Its future might be shrouded in gloom, and the hope of its prophets go out in sorrow. There is consolation in the thought that America is young. Great streams are not easily turned from channels, worn deep in the course of ages. They may sometimes rise in quiet and stately majesty, and inundate the land, refreshing and fertilizing the earth with their mysterious properties. They may also rise in wrath and fury, and bear away, on their angry waves, the accumulated wealth of years of toil and hardship. They, however, gradually flow back to the same old channel, and flow on as serenely as ever. But, while the river may not be turned aside, it may dry up, and leave nothing behind but the withered branch, and the unsightly rock, to howl in the abyss-sweeping wind, the sad tale of departed glory. As with rivers so with nations.

Fellow-citizens, I shall not presume to dwell at length on the associations that cluster about this day. The simple story of it is that, 76 years ago, the people of this country were British subjects. The style and title of your "sovereign people" (in which you now glory) was not then born. You were under the British Crown . Your fathers esteemed the English Government as the home government; and England as the fatherland. This home government, you know, although a considerable distance from your home, did, in the exercise of its parental prerogatives, impose upon its colonial children, such restraints, burdens and limitations, as, in its mature judgment, it deemed wise, right and proper.

But, your fathers, who had not adopted the fashionable idea of this day, of the infallibility of government, and the absolute character of its acts, presumed to differ from the home government in respect to the wisdom and the justice of some of those burdens and restraints. They went so far in their excitement as to pronounce the measures of government unjust, unreasonable, and oppressive, and altogether such as ought not to be quietly submitted to. I scarcely need say, fellow citizens, that my opinion of those measures fully accords with that of your fathers. Such a declaration of agreement on my part would not be worth much to anybody. It would, certainly, prove nothing, as to what part I might have taken, had I lived during the great controversy of 1776. To say now that America was right, and England wrong, is exceedingly easy. Everybody can say it; the dastard, not less than the noble brave, can flippantly discant on the tyranny of England towards the American Colonies. It is fashionable to do so; but there was a time when to pronounce against England, and in favor of the cause of the colonies, tried men's souls. They who did so were accounted in their day, plotters of mischief, agitators and rebels, dangerous men. To side with the right, against the wrong, with the weak against the strong, and with the oppressed against the oppressor! here lies the merit, and the one which, of all others, seems unfashionable in our day. The cause of liberty may be stabbed by the men who glory in the deeds of your fathers. But, to proceed.

Feeling themselves harshly and unjustly treated by the home government, your fathers, like men of honesty, and men of spirit, earnestly sought redress. They petitioned and remonstrated; they did so in a decorous, respectful, and loyal manner. Their conduct was wholly unexceptionable. This, however, did not answer the purpose. They saw themselves treated with sovereign indifference, coldness and scorn. Yet they persevered. They were not the men to look back.

As the sheet anchor takes a firmer hold, when the ship is tossed by the storm, so did the cause of your fathers grow stronger, as it breasted the chilling blasts of kingly displeasure. The greatest and best of British statesmen admitted its justice, and the loftiest eloquence of the British Senate came to its support. But, with that blindness which seems to be the unvarying characteristic of tyrants, since Pharaoh and his hosts were drowned in the Red Sea, the British Government persisted in the exactions complained of.

The madness of this course, we believe, is admitted now, even by England; but we fear the lesson is wholly lost on our present ruler.

Oppression makes a wise man mad. Your fathers were wise men, and if they did not go mad, they became restive under this treatment. They felt themselves the victims of grievous wrongs, wholly incurable in their colonial capacity. With brave men there is always a remedy for oppression. Just here, the idea of a total separation of the colonies from the crown was born! It was a startling idea, much more so, than we, at this distance of time, regard it. The timid and the prudent (as has been intimated) of that day, were, of course, shocked and alarmed by it. Such people lived then, had lived before, and will, probably, ever have a place on this planet; and their course, in respect to any great change, (no matter how great the good to be attained, or the wrong to be redressed by it), may be calculated with as much precision as can be the course of the stars. They hate all changes, but silver, gold and copper change! Of this sort of change they are always strongly in favor.

These people were called Tories in the days of your fathers; and the appellation, probably, conveyed the same idea that is meant by a more modern, though a somewhat less euphonious term, which we often find in our papers, applied to some of our old politicians.

Their opposition to the then dangerous thought was earnest and powerful; but, amid all their terror and affrighted vociferations against it, the alarming and revolutionary idea moved on, and the country with it.

On the second of July, 1776, the old Continental Congress, to the dismay of the lovers of ease, and the worshipers of property, clothed that dreadful idea with all the authority of national sanction. They did so in the form of a resolution; and as we seldom hit upon resolutions, drawn up in our day whose transparency is at all equal to this, it may refresh your minds and help my story if I read it.

[We] solemnly publish and declare, That these United Colonies are, and of right, ought to be free and Independent States; that they are Absolved from all Allegiance to the British Crown; and that all political connection between them and the State of Great Britain is and ought to be [totally] dissolved.

Citizens, your fathers made good that resolution. They succeeded; and to-day you reap the fruits of their success. The freedom gained is yours; and you, therefore, may properly celebrate this anniversary. The 4th of July is the first great fact in your nation's history —the very ring—bolt in the chain of your yet undeveloped destiny.

Pride and patriotism, not less than gratitude, prompt you to celebrate and to hold it in perpetual remembrance. I have said that the Declaration of Independence is the ring-bolt to the chain of your nation's destiny; so, indeed, I regard it. The principles contained in that instrument are saving principles. Stand by those principles, be true to them on all occasions, in all places, against all foes, and at whatever cost.

From the round top of your ship of state, dark and threatening clouds may be seen. Heavy billows, like mountains in the distance, disclose to the leeward huge forms of flinty rocks! That bolt drawn, that chain broken, and all is lost. Cling to this day—cling to it, and to its principles, with the grasp of a storm-tossed mariner to a spar at midnight.

The coming into being of a nation, in any circumstances, is an interesting event. But, besides general considerations, there were peculiar circumstances which make the advent of this republic an event of special attractiveness.

The whole scene, as I look back to it, was simple, dignified and sublime.

The population of the country, at the time, stood at the insignificant number of three millions. The country was poor in the munitions of war. The population was weak and scattered, and the country a wilderness unsubdued. There were then no means of concert and combination, such as exist now. Neither steam nor lightning had then been reduced to order and discipline. From the Potomac to the Delaware was a journey of many days. Under these, and innumerable other disadvantages, your fathers declared for liberty and independence and triumphed.

Fellow Citizens, I am not wanting in respect for the fathers of this republic. The signers of the Declaration of Independence were brave men. They were great men too—great enough to give fame to a great age. It does not often happen to a nation to raise, at one time, such a number of truly great men. The point from which I am compelled to view them is not, certainly, the most favorable; and yet I cannot contemplate their great deeds with less than admiration. They were statesmen, patriots and heroes, and for the good they did, and the principles they contended for, I will unite with you to honor their memory.

They loved their country better than their own private interests; and, though this is not the highest form of human excellence, all will concede that it is a rare virtue, and that when it is exhibited, it ought to command respect. He who will, intelligently, lay down his life for his country, is a man whom it is not in human nature to despise. Your fathers staked their lives, their fortunes, and their sacred honor, on the cause of their country. In their admiration of liberty, they lost sight of all other interests.

They were peace men; but they preferred revolution to peaceful submission to bondage. They were quiet men; but they did not shrink from agitating against oppression. They showed forbearance; but that they knew its limits. They believed in order; but not in the order of tyranny. With them, nothing was "settled" that was not right. With them, justice, liberty and humanity were "final;" not slavery and oppression. You may well cherish the memory of such men. They were great in their day and generation. Their solid manhood stands out the more as we contrast it with these degenerate times.

How circumspect, exact and proportionate were all their movements! How unlike the politicians of an hour! Their statesmanship looked beyond the passing moment, and stretched away in strength into the distant future. They seized upon eternal principles, and set a glorious example in their defense. Mark them!

Fully appreciating the hardship to be encountered, firmly believing in the right of their cause, honorably inviting the scrutiny of an on-looking world, reverently appealing to heaven to attest their sincerity, soundly comprehending the solemn responsibility they were about to assume, wisely measuring the terrible odds against them, your fathers, the fathers of this republic, did, most deliberately, under the inspiration of a glorious patriotism, and with a sublime faith in the great principles of justice and freedom, lay deep the corner-stone of the national superstructure, which has risen and still rises in grandeur around you.

Of this fundamental work, this day is the anniversary. Our eyes are met with demonstrations of joyous enthusiasm. Banners and pennants wave exultingly on the breeze. The din of business, too, is hushed. Even Mammon seems to have quitted his grasp on this day. The ear-piercing fife and the stirring drum unite their accents with the ascending peal of a thousand church bells. Prayers are made, hymns are sung, and sermons are preached in honor of this day; while the quick martial tramp of a great and multitudinous nation, echoed back by all the hills, valleys and mountains of a vast continent, bespeak the occasion one of thrilling and universal interests nation's jubilee.

Friends and citizens, I need not enter further into the causes which led to this anniversary. Many of you understand them better than I do. You could instruct me in regard to them. That is a branch of knowledge in which you feel, perhaps, a much deeper interest than your speaker. The causes which led to the separation of the colonies from the British crown have never lacked for a tongue. They have all been taught in your common schools, narrated at your firesides, unfolded from your pulpits, and thundered from your legislative halls, and are as familiar to you as household words. They form the staple of your national poetry and eloquence.

I remember also that as a people Americans are remarkably familiar with all facts which make in their own favor. This is esteemed by some as a national trait—perhaps a national weakness. It is a fact, that whatever makes for the wealth or for the reputation of Americans, and can be had cheap will be found by Americans. I shall not be charged with slandering Americans if I say I think the American side of any question may be safely left in American hands.

I leave, therefore, the great deeds of your fathers to other gentlemen whose claim to have been regularly descended will be less likely to be disputed than mine!

My business, if I have any here to-day, is with the present. The accepted time with God and his cause is the ever-living now.

Trust no future, however pleasant, Let the dead past bury its dead; Act, act in the living present, Heart within, and God overhead.

We have to do with the past only as we can make it useful to the present and to the future. To all inspiring motives, to noble deeds which can be gained from the past, we are welcome. But now is the time, the important time. Your fathers have lived, died, and have done their work, and have done much of it well. You live and must die, and you must do your work. You have no right to enjoy a child's share in the labor of your fathers, unless your children are to be blest by your labors. You have no right to wear out and waste the hard-earned fame of your fathers to cover your indolence. Sydney Smith tells us that men seldom eulogize the wisdom and virtues of their fathers, but to excuse some folly or wickedness of their own. This truth is not a doubtful one. There are illustrations of it near and remote, ancient and modern. It was fashionable, hundreds of years ago, for the children of Jacob to boast, we have "Abraham to our father," when they had long lost Abraham's faith and spirit. That people contented themselves under the shadow of Abraham's great name, while they repudiated the deeds which made his name great. Need I remind you that a similar thing is being done all over this country to-day? Need I tell you that the Jews are not the only people who built the tombs of the prophets, and garnished the sepulchres of the righteous? Washington could not die till he had broken the chains of his slaves. Yet his monument is built up by the price of human blood, and the traders in the bodies and souls of men, shout —"We have Washington to our father."—Alas! that it should be so; yet so it is.

The evil that men do, lives after them, The good is oft' interred with their bones.

Fellow-citizens, pardon me, allow me to ask, why am I called upon to speak here to-day? What have I, or those I represent, to do with your national independence? Are the great principles of political freedom and of natural justice, embodied in that Declaration of Independence, extended to us? and am I, therefore, called upon to bring our humble offering to the national altar, and to confess the benefits and express devout gratitude for the blessings resulting from your independence to us?

Would to God, both for your sakes and ours, that an affirmative answer could be truthfully returned to these questions! Then would my task be light, and my burden easy and delightful. For who is there so cold, that a nation's sympathy could not warm him? Who so obdurate and dead to the claims of gratitude, that would not thankfully acknowledge such priceless benefits? Who so stolid and selfish, that would not give his voice to swell the hallelujahs of a nation's jubilee, when the chains of servitude had been tom from his limbs? I am not that man. In a case like that, the dumb might eloquently speak, and the "lame man leap as an hart."

But, such is not the state of the case. I say it with a sad sense of the disparity between us. I am not included within the pale of this glorious anniversary! Your high independence only reveals the immeasurable distance between us. The blessings in which you, this day, rejoice, are not enjoyed in common. The rich inheritance of justice, liberty, prosperity and independence, bequeathed by your fathers, is shared by you, not by me. The sunlight that brought life and healing to you, has brought stripes and death to me. This Fourth of July is yours, not mine. You may rejoice, I must mourn. To drag a man in fetters into the grand illuminated temple of liberty, and call upon him to join you in joyous anthems, were inhuman mockery and sacrilegious irony. Do you mean, citizens, to mock me, by asking me to speak to-day? If so, there is a parallel to your conduct. And let me warn you that it is dangerous to copy the example of a nation whose crimes, lowering up to heaven, were thrown down by the breath of the Almighty, burying that nation in irrecoverable ruin! I can to-day take up the plaintive lament of a peeled and woe-smitten people!

"By the rivers of Babylon, there we sat down. Yea! we wept when we remembered Zion. We hanged our harps upon the willows in the midst thereof. For there, they that carried us away captive, required of us a song; and they who wasted us required of us mirth, saying, Sing us one of the songs of Zion. How can we sing the Lord's song in a strange land? If I forget thee, O Jerusalem, let my right hand forget her cunning. If I do not remember thee, let my tongue cleave to the roof of my mouth."

Fellow-citizens; above your national, tumultuous joy, I hear the mournful wail of millions! whose chains, heavy and grievous yesterday, are, to-day, rendered more intolerable by the jubilee shouts that reach them. If I do forget, if I do not faithfully remember those bleeding children of sorrow this day, "may my right hand forget her cunning, and may my tongue cleave to the roof of my mouth!" To forget them, to pass lightly over their wrongs, and to chime in with the popular theme, would be treason most scandalous and shocking, and would make me a reproach before God and the world. My subject, then fellow-citizens, is American slavery. I shall see, this day, and its popular characteristics, from the slave's point of view. Standing, there, identified with the American bondman, making his wrongs mine, I do not hesitate to declare, with all my soul, that the character and conduct of this nation never looked blacker to me than on this 4th of July! Whether we turn to the declarations of the past, or to the professions of the present, the conduct of the nation seems equally hideous and revolting. America is false to the past, false to the present, and solemnly binds herself to be false to the future. Standing with God and the crushed and bleeding slave on this occasion, I will, in the name of humanity which is outraged, in the name of liberty which is fettered, in the name of the constitution and the Bible, which are disregarded and trampled upon, dare to call in question and to denounce, with all the emphasis I can command, everything that serves to perpetuate slavery—the great sin and shame of America! "I will not equivocate; I will not excuse;" I will use the severest language I can command; and yet not one word shall escape me that any man, whose judgment is not blinded by prejudice, or who is not at heart a slaveholder, shall not confess to be fight and just. But I fancy I hear some one of my audience say, it is just in this circumstance that you and your brother abolitionists fail to make a favorable impression on the public mind. Would you argue more, and denounce less, would you persuade more, and rebuke less, your cause would be much more likely to succeed. But, I submit, where all is plain there is nothing to be argued. What point in the anti-slavery creed would you have me argue? On what branch of the subject do the people of this country need light? Must I undertake to prove that the slave is a man? That point is conceded already. Nobody doubts it. The slaveholders themselves acknowledge it in the enactment of laws for their government. They acknowledge it when they punish disobedience on the part of the slave. There are seventy-two crimes in the State of Virginia, which, if committed by a black man, (no matter how ignorant he be), subject him to the punishment of death; while only two of the same crimes will subject a white man to the like punishment. What is this but the acknowledgement that the slave is a moral, intellectual and responsible being? The manhood of the slave is conceded. It is admitted in the fact that Southern statute books are covered with enactments forbidding, under severe fines and penalties, the teaching of the slave to read or to write. When you can point to any such laws, in reference to the beasts of the field, then I may consent to argue the manhood of the slave. When the dogs in your streets, when the fowls of the air, when the cattle on your hills, when the fish of the sea, and the reptiles that crawl, shall be unable to distinguish the slave from a brute, their will I argue with you that the slave is a man!

For the present, it is enough to affirm the equal manhood of the Negro race. Is it not astonishing that, while we are ploughing, planting and reaping, using all kinds of mechanical tools, erecting houses, constructing bridges, building ships, working in metals of brass, iron, copper, silver and gold; that, while we are reading, writing and cyphering, acting as clerks, merchants and secretaries, having among us lawyers, doctors, ministers, poets, authors, editors, orators and teachers; that, while we are engaged in all manner of enterprises common to other men, digging gold in California, capturing the whale in the Pacific, feeding sheep and cattle on the hillside, living, moving, acting, thinking, planning, living in families as husbands, wives and children, and, above all, confessing and worshipping the Christian's God, and looking hopefully for life and immortality beyond the grave, we are called upon to prove that we are men!

Would you have me argue that man is entitled to liberty? that he is the rightful owner of his own body? You have already declared it. Must I argue the wrongfulness of slavery? Is that a question for Republicans? Is it to be settled by the rules of logic and argumentation, as a matter beset with great difficulty, involving a doubtful application of the principle of justice, hard to be understood? How should I look to-day, in the presence of Americans, dividing, and subdividing a discourse, to show that men have a natural right to freedom? speaking of it relatively, and positively, negatively, and affirmatively. To do so, would be to make myself ridiculous, and to offer an insult to your understanding. There is not a man beneath the canopy of heaven, that does not know that slavery is wrong for him.

What, am I to argue that it is wrong to make men brutes, to rob them of their liberty, to work them without wages, to keep them ignorant of their relations to their fellow men, to beat them with sticks, to flay their flesh with the lash, to load their limbs with irons, to hunt them with dogs, to sell them at auction, to sunder their families, to knock out their teeth, to bum their flesh, to starve them into obedience and submission to their masters? Must I argue that a system thus marked with blood and stained with pollution is wrong? No! I will not. I have better employments for my time and strength than such arguments would imply.

What, then, remains to be argued? Is it that slavery is not divine; that God did not establish it; that our doctors of divinity are mistaken? There is blasphemy in the thought. That which is inhuman, cannot be divine! Who can reason on such a proposition? They that can, may; I cannot. The time for such argument is past.

At a time like this, scorching irony, not convincing argument, is needed. O! had I the ability, and could I reach the nation's ear, I would, to-day, pour out a fiery stream of biting ridicule, blasting reproach, withering sarcasm, and stern rebuke. For it is not light that is needed, but fire; it is not the gentle shower, but thunder. We need the storm, the whirlwind, and the earthquake. The feeling of the nation must be quickened; the conscience of the nation must be roused; the propriety of the nation must be startled; the hypocrisy of the nation must be exposed; and its crimes against God and man must be proclaimed and denounced.

What, to the American slave, is your Fourth of July? I answer: a day that reveals to him, more than all other days in the year, the gross injustice and cruelly to which he is the constant victim. To him, your celebration is a sham; your boasted liberty, an unholy license; your national greatness, swelling vanity; your sounds of rejoicing are empty and heartless; your denunciations of tyrants, brass fronted impudence; your shouts of liberty and equality, hollow mockery; your prayers and hymns, your sermons and thanksgivings, with all your religious parade, and solemnity, are, to him, mere bombast, fraud, deception, impiety, and hypocrisy—a thin veil to cover up crimes which would disgrace a nation of savages. There is not a nation on the earth guilty of practices, more shocking and bloody, than are the people of these United States, at this very hour.

Go where you may, search where you will, roam through all the monarchies and despotisms of the old world, travel through South America, search out every abuse, and when you have found the last, lay your facts by the side of the everyday practices of this nation, and you will say with me, that, for revolting barbarity and shameless hypocrisy, America reigns without a rival. Take the American slave-trade, which, we are told by the papers, is especially prosperous just now. Ex-Senator Benton tells us that the price of men was never higher than now. He mentions the fact to show that slavery is in no danger. This trade is one of the peculiarities of American institutions. It is carried on in all the large towns and cities in one-half of this confederacy; and millions are pocketed every year, by dealers in this horrid traffic. In several states, this trade is a chief source of wealth. It is called (in contradistinction to the foreign slave-trade) "the internal slave trade." It is, probably, called so, too, in order to divert from it the horror with which the foreign slave-trade is contemplated. That trade has long since been denounced by this government, as piracy. It has been denounced with burning words, from the high places of the nation, as an execrable traffic. To arrest it, to put an end to it, this nation keeps a squadron, at immense cost, on the coast of Africa. Everywhere, in this country, it is safe to speak of this foreign slave-trade, as a most inhuman traffic, opposed alike to the laws of God and of man. The duty to extirpate and destroy it, is admitted even by our doctors of divinity. In order to put an end to it, some of these last have consented that their colored brethren (nominally free) should leave this country, and establish themselves on the western coast of Africa! It is, however, a notable fact that, while so much execration is poured out by Americans upon those engaged in the foreign slave-trade, the men engaged in the slave-trade between the states pass without condemnation, and their business is deemed honorable.

Behold the practical operation of this internal slave-trade, the American slave-trade, sustained by American politics and America religion. Here you will see men and women reared like swine for the market. You know what is a swine-drover? I will show you a man-drover. They inhabit all our Southern States. They perambulate the country, and crowd the highways of the nation, with droves of human stock. You will see one of these human flesh-jobbers, armed with pistol, whip and bowie-knife, driving a company of a hundred men, women, and children, from the Potomac to the slave market at New Orleans. These wretched people are to be sold singly, or in lots, to suit purchasers. They are food for the cotton-field, and the deadly sugar-mill. Mark the sad procession, as it moves wearily along, and the inhuman wretch who drives them. Hear his savage yells and his blood-chilling oaths, as he hurries on his affrighted captives! There, see the old man, with locks thinned and gray. Cast one glance, if you please, upon that young mother, whose shoulders are bare to the scorching sun, her briny tears falling on the brow of the babe in her arms. See, too, that girl of thirteen, weeping, yes! weeping, as she thinks of the mother from whom she has been torn! The drove moves tardily. Heat and sorrow have nearly consumed their strength; suddenly you hear a quick snap, like the discharge of a rifle; the fetters clank, and the chain rattles simultaneously; your ears are saluted with a scream, that seems to have torn its way to the center of your soul! The crack you heard, was the sound of the slave-whip; the scream you heard, was from the woman you saw with the babe. Her speed had faltered under the weight of her child and her chains! that gash on her shoulder tells her to move on. Follow the drove to New Orleans. Attend the auction; see men examined like horses; see the forms of women rudely and brutally exposed to the shocking gaze of American slave-buyers. See this drove sold and separated forever; and never forget the deep, sad sobs that arose from that scattered multitude. Tell me citizens, where, under the sun, you can witness a spectacle more fiendish and shocking. Yet this is but a glance at the American slave-trade, as it exists, at this moment, in the ruling part of the United States.

I was born amid such sights and scenes. To me the American slave-trade is a terrible reality. When a child, my soul was often pierced with a sense of its horrors. I lived on Philpot Street, Fell's Point, Baltimore, and have watched from the wharves, the slave ships in the Basin, anchored from the shore, with their cargoes of human flesh, waiting for favorable winds to waft them down the Chesapeake. There was, at that time, a grand slave mart kept at the head of Pratt Street, by Austin Woldfolk. His agents were sent into every town and county in Maryland, announcing their arrival, through the papers, and on flaming hand-bills headed "Cash for Negroes." These men were generally well dressed men, and very captivating in their manners. Ever ready to drink, to treat, and to gamble. The fate of many a slave has depended upon the turn of a single card; and many a child has been snatched from the arms of its mother by bargains arranged in a state of brutal drunkenness.

The flesh-mongers gather up their victims by dozens, and drive them, chained, to the general depot at Baltimore. When a sufficient number have been collected here, a ship is chartered, for the purpose of conveying the forlorn crew to Mobile, or to New Orleans. From the slave prison to the ship, they are usually driven in the darkness of night; for since the antislavery agitation, a certain caution is observed.

In the deep, still darkness of midnight I have been often aroused by the dead heavy footsteps, and the piteous cries of the chained gangs that passed our door. The anguish of my boyish heart was intense; and I was often consoled, when speaking to my mistress in the morning, to hear her say that the custom was very wicked; that she hated to hear the rattle of the chains, and the heart-rending cries. I was glad to find one who sympathized with me in my horror. Fellow-citizens, this murderous traffic is, to-day, in active operation in this boasted republic. In the solitude of my spirit, I see clouds of dust raised on the highways of the South; I see the bleeding footsteps; I hear the doleful wail of fettered humanity, on the way to the slave markets, where the victims are to be sold like horses, sheep and swine, knocked off to the highest bidder. There I see the tenderest ties ruthlessly broken, to gratify the lust, caprice and rapacity of the buyers and sellers of men. My soul sickens at the sight.

Is this the land your Fathers loved, The freedom which they toiled to win? Is this the earth whereon they moved? Are these the graves they slumber in?

But a still more inhuman, disgraceful, and scandalous state of things remains to be presented. By an act of the American Congress, not yet two years old, slavery has been nationalized in its most horrible and revolting form. By that act, Mason & Dixon's line has been obliterated; New York has become as Virginia; and the power to hold, hunt, and sell men, women, and children as slaves remains no longer a mere state institution, but is now an institution of the whole United States. The power is co-extensive with the Star-Spangled Banner and American Christianity. Where these go, may also go the merciless slave-hunter. Where these are, man is not sacred. He is a bird for the sportsman's gun. By that most foul and fiendish of all human decrees, the liberty and person of every man are put in peril. Your broad republican domain is hunting ground for men. Not for thieves and robbers, enemies of society, merely, but for men guilty of no crime. Your lawmakers have commanded all good citizens to engage in this hellish sport. Your President, your Secretary of State, your lords, nobles and ecclesiastics enforce, as a duty you owe to your free and glorious country, and to your God, that you do this accursed thing. Not fewer than forty Americans have, within the past two years, been hunted down and, without a moment's warning, hurried away in chains, and consigned to slavery and excruciating torture. Some of these have had wives and children, dependent on them for bread; but of this, no account was made. The right of the hunter to his prey stands superior to the right of marriage, and to all rights in this republic, the rights of God included! For black men there are neither law, justice, humanity, not religion. The Fugitive Slave Law makes makes mercy to them a crime; and bribes the judge who tries them. An American judge gets ten dollars for every victim he consigns to slavery, and five, when he fails to do so. The oath of any two villains is sufficient, under this hell-black enactment, to send the most pious and exemplary black man into the remorseless jaws of slavery! His own testimony is nothing. He can bring no witnesses for himself. The minister of American justice is bound by the law to hear but one side; and that side, is the side of the oppressor. Let this damning fact be perpetually told. Let it be thundered around the world, that, in tyrant-killing, king-hating, people-loving, democratic, Christian America, the seats of justice are filled with judges, who hold their offices under an open and palpable bribe, and are bound, in deciding in the case of a man's liberty, to hear only his accusers!

In glaring violation of justice, in shameless disregard of the forms of administering law, in cunning arrangement to entrap the defenseless, and in diabolical intent, this Fugitive Slave Law stands alone in the annals of tyrannical legislation. I doubt if there be another nation on the globe, having the brass and the baseness to put such a law on the statute-book. If any man in this assembly thinks differently from me in this matter, and feels able to disprove my statements, I will gladly confront him at any suitable time and place he may select.

I take this law to be one of the grossest infringements of Christian Liberty, and, if the churches and ministers of our country were not stupidly blind, or most wickedly indifferent, they, too, would so regard it.

At the very moment that they are thanking God for the enjoyment of civil and religious liberty, and for the right to worship God according to the dictates of their own consciences, they are utterly silent in respect to a law which robs religion of its chief significance, and makes it utterly worthless to a world lying in wickedness. Did this law concern the "mint, anise and cummin" —abridge the fight to sing psalms, to partake of the sacrament, or to engage in any of the ceremonies of religion, it would be smitten by the thunder of a thousand pulpits. A general shout would go up from the church, demanding repeal, repeal, instant repeal! And it would go hard with that politician who presumed to solicit the votes of the people without inscribing this motto on his banner. Further, if this demand were not complied with, another Scotland would be added to the history of religious liberty, and the stern old Covenanters would be thrown into the shade. A John Knox would be seen at every church door, and heard from every pulpit, and Fillmore would have no more quarter than was shown by Knox, to the beautiful, but treacherous queen Mary of Scotland. The fact that the church of our country, (with fractional exceptions), does not esteem "the Fugitive Slave Law" as a declaration of war against religious liberty, implies that that church regards religion simply as a form of worship, an empty ceremony, and not a vital principle, requiring active benevolence, justice, love and good will towards man. It esteems sacrifice above mercy; psalm-singing above right doing; solemn meetings above practical righteousness. A worship that can be conducted by persons who refuse to give shelter to the houseless, to give bread to the hungry, clothing to the naked, and who enjoin obedience to a law forbidding these acts of mercy, is a curse, not a blessing to mankind. The Bible addresses all such persons as "scribes, Pharisees, hypocrites, who pay tithe of mint, anise, and cummin, and have omitted the weightier matters of the law, judgment, mercy and faith." But the church of this country is not only indifferent to the wrongs of die slave, it actually takes sides with the oppressors. It has made itself the bulwark of American slavery, and the shield of American slave-hunters. Many of its most eloquent Divines. who stand as the very lights of the church, have shamelessly given the sanction of religion and the Bible to the whole slave system. They have taught that man may, properly, be a slave; that the relation of master and slave is ordained of God; that to send back an escaped bondman to his master is clearly the duty of all the followers of the Lord Jesus Christ; and this horrible blasphemy is palmed off upon the world for Christianity.

For my part, I would say, Welcome infidelity! welcome atheism! welcome anything—in preference to the gospel, as preached by those divines. They convert the very name of religion into an engine of tyranny, and barbarous cruelty, and serve to confirm more infidels, in this age, than all the infidel writings of Thomas Paine, Voltaire, and Bolingbroke, put together, have done! These ministers make religion a cold and flinty-hearted thing, having neither principles of right action, nor bowels of compassion. They strip the love of God of its beauty, and leave the throng of religion a huge, horrible, repulsive form. It is a religion for oppressors, tyrants, man-stealers, and thugs. It is not that "pure and undefiled religion" which is from above, and which is "first pure, then peaceable, easy to be entreated, full of mercy and good fruits, without partiality and without hypocrisy." But a religion which favors the rich against the poor; which exalts the proud above the humble; which divides mankind into two classes, tyrants and slaves; which says to the man in chains, stay there; and to the oppressor, oppress on; it is a religion which may be professed and enjoyed by all the robbers and enslavers of mankind; it makes God a respecter of persons, denies his fatherhood of the race, and tramples in the dust the great truth of the brotherhood of man. All this we affirm to be true of the popular church, and the popular worship of our land and nation—a religion, a church, and a worship which, on the authority of inspired wisdom, we pronounce to be an abomination in the sight of God. In the language of Isaiah, the American church might be well addressed, "Bring no more vain ablations; incense is an abomination unto me: the new moons and Sabbaths, the calling of assemblies, I cannot away with; it is iniquity even the solemn meeting. Your new moons and your appointed feasts my soul hateth. They are a trouble to me; I am weary to bear them; and when ye spread forth your hands I will hide mine eyes from you. Yea! when ye make many prayers, I will not hear. Your hands are full of blood; cease to do evil, learn to do well; seek judgment; relieve the oppressed; judge for the fatherless; plead for the widow."

The American church is guilty, when viewed in connection with what it is doing to uphold slavery; but it is superlatively guilty when viewed in connection with its ability to abolish slavery.

The sin of which it is guilty is one of omission as well as of commission. Albert Barnes but uttered what the common sense of every man at all observant of the actual state of the case will receive as truth, when he declared that "There is no power out of the church that could sustain slavery an hour, if it were not sustained in it."

Let the religious press, the pulpit, the Sunday school, the conference meeting, the great ecclesiastical, missionary, Bible and tract associations of the land array their immense powers against slavery and slave-holding; and the whole system of crime and blood would be scattered to the winds; and that they do not do this involves them in the most awful responsibility of which the mind can conceive.

In prosecuting the anti-slavery enterprise, we have been asked to spare the church, to spare the ministry; but how, we ask, could such a thing be done? We are met on the threshold of our efforts for the redemption of the slave, by the church and ministry of the country, in battle arrayed against us; and we are compelled to fight or flee. From what quarter, I beg to know, has proceeded a fire so deadly upon our ranks, during the last two years, as from the Northern pulpit? As the champions of oppressors, the chosen men of American theology have appeared—men, honored for their so-called piety, and their real learning. The Lords of Buffalo, the Springs of New York, the Lathrops of Auburn, the Coxes and Spencers of Brooklyn, the Gannets and Sharps of Boston, the Deweys of Washington, and other great religious lights of the land, have, in utter denial of the authority of Him, by whom the professed to he called to the ministry, deliberately taught us, against the example or the Hebrews and against the remonstrance of the Apostles, they teach "that we ought to obey man's law before the law of God."

My spirit wearies of such blasphemy; and how such men can be supported, as the "standing types and representatives of Jesus Christ," is a mystery which I leave others to penetrate. In speaking of the American church, however, let it be distinctly understood that I mean the great mass of the religious organizations of our land. There are exceptions, and I thank God that there are. Noble men may be found, scattered all over these Northern States, of whom Henry Ward Beecher of Brooklyn, Samuel J. May of Syracuse, and my esteemed friend [Rev. R. R. Raymond] on the platform, are shining examples; and let me say further, that upon these men lies the duty to inspire our ranks with high religious faith and zeal, and to cheer us on in the great mission of the slave's redemption from his chains.

One is struck with the difference between the attitude of the American church towards the anti-slavery movement, and that occupied by the churches in England towards a similar movement in that country. There, the church, true to its mission of ameliorating, elevating, and improving the condition of mankind, came forward promptly, bound up the wounds of the West Indian slave, and restored him to his liberty. There, the question of emancipation was a high[ly] religious question. It was demanded, in the name of humanity, and according to the law of the living God. The Sharps, the Clarksons, the Wilberforces, the Buxtons, and Burchells and the Knibbs, were alike famous for their piety, and for their philanthropy. The anti-slavery movement there was not an anti-church movement, for the reason that the church took its full share in prosecuting that movement: and the anti-slavery movement in this country will cease to be an anti-church movement, when the church of this country shall assume a favorable instead or a hostile position towards that movement.

Americans! your republican politics, not less than your republican religion, are flagrantly inconsistent. You boast of your love of liberty, your superior civilization, and your pure Christianity, while the whole political power of the nation (as embodied in the two great political parties) is solemnly pledged to support and perpetuate the enslavement of three millions of your countrymen. You hurl your anathemas at the crowned headed tyrants of Russia and Austria, and pride yourselves on your Democratic institutions, while you yourselves consent to be the mere tools and bodyguards of the tyrants of Virginia and Carolina. You invite to your shores fugitives of oppression from abroad, honor them with banquets, greet them with ovations, cheer them, toast them, salute them, protect them, and pour out your money to them like water; but the fugitives from your own land you advertise, hunt, arrest, shoot and kill. You glory in your refinement and your universal education yet you maintain a system as barbarous and dreadful as ever stained the character of a nation—a system begun in avarice, supported in pride, and perpetuated in cruelty. You shed tears over fallen Hungary, and make the sad story of her wrongs the theme of your poets, statesmen and orators, till your gallant sons are ready to fly to arms to vindicate her cause against her oppressors; but, in regard to the ten thousand wrongs of the American slave, you would enforce the strictest silence, and would hail him as an enemy of the nation who dares to make those wrongs the subject of public discourse! You are all on fire at the mention of liberty for France or for Ireland; but are as cold as an iceberg at the thought of liberty for the enslaved of America. You discourse eloquently on the dignity of labor; yet, you sustain a system which, in its very essence, casts a stigma upon labor. You can bare your bosom to the storm of British artillery to throw off a threepenny tax on tea; and yet wring the last hard-earned farthing from the grasp of the black laborers of your country. You profess to believe "that, of one blood, God made all nations of men to dwell on the face of all the earth," and hath commanded all men, everywhere to love one another; yet you notoriously hate, (and glory in your hatred), all men whose skins are not colored like your own. You declare, before the world, and are understood by the world to declare, that you "hold these truths to be self evident, that all men are created equal; and are endowed by their Creator with certain inalienable rights; and that, among these are, life, liberty, and the pursuit of happiness;" and yet, you hold securely, in a bondage which, according to your own Thomas Jefferson, "is worse than ages of that which your fathers rose in rebellion to oppose," a seventh part of the inhabitants of your country.

Fellow-citizens! I will not enlarge further on your national inconsistencies. The existence of slavery in this country brands your republicanism as a sham, your humanity as a base pretence, and your Christianity as a lie. It destroys your moral power abroad; it corrupts your politicians at home. It saps the foundation of religion; it makes your name a hissing, and a by word to a mocking earth. It is the antagonistic force in your government, the only thing that seriously disturbs and endangers your Union. It fetters your progress; it is the enemy of improvement, the deadly foe of education; it fosters pride; it breeds insolence; it promotes vice; it shelters crime; it is a curse to the earth that supports it; and yet, you cling to it, as if it were the sheet anchor of all your hopes. Oh! be warned! be warned! a horrible reptile is coiled up in your nation's bosom; the venomous creature is nursing at the tender breast of your youthful republic; for the love of God, tear away, and fling from you the hideous monster, and let the weight of twenty millions crush and destroy it forever!

But it is answered in reply to all this, that precisely what I have now denounced is, in fact, guaranteed and sanctioned by the Constitution of the United States; that the right to hold and to hunt slaves is a part of that Constitution framed by the illustrious Fathers of this Republic. Then, I dare to affirm, notwithstanding all I have said before, your fathers stooped, basely stooped

To palter with us in a double sense: And keep the word of promise to the ear, But break it to the heart.

And instead of being the honest men I have before declared them to be, they were the veriest imposters that ever practiced on mankind. This is the inevitable conclusion, and from it there is no escape. But I differ from those who charge this baseness on the framers of the Constitution of the United States. It is a slander upon their memory, at least, so I believe. There is not time now to argue the constitutional question at length – nor have I the ability to discuss it as it ought to be discussed. The subject has been handled with masterly power by Lysander Spooner, Esq., by William Goodell, by Samuel E. Sewall, Esq., and last, though not least, by Gerritt Smith, Esq. These gentlemen have, as I think, fully and clearly vindicated the Constitution from any design to support slavery for an hour.

Fellow-citizens! there is no matter in respect to which, the people of the North have allowed themselves to be so ruinously imposed upon, as that of the pro-slavery character of the Constitution. In that instrument I hold there is neither warrant, license, nor sanction of the hateful thing; but, interpreted as it ought to be interpreted, the Constitution is a glorious liberty document. Read its preamble, consider its purposes. Is slavery among them? Is it at the gateway? or is it in the temple? It is neither. While I do not intend to argue this question on the present occasion, let me ask, if it be not somewhat singular that, if the Constitution were intended to be, by its framers and adopters, a slave-holding instrument, why neither slavery, slaveholding, nor slave can anywhere be found in it. What would be thought of an instrument, drawn up, legally drawn up, for the purpose of entitling the city of Rochester to a track of land, in which no mention of land was made? Now, there are certain rules of interpretation, for the proper understanding of all legal instruments. These rules are well established. They are plain, common-sense rules, such as you and I, and all of us, can understand and apply, without having passed years in the study of law. I scout the idea that the question of the constitutionality or unconstitutionality of slavery is not a question for the people. I hold that every American citizen has a fight to form an opinion of the constitution, and to propagate that opinion, and to use all honorable means to make his opinion the prevailing one. Without this fight, the liberty of an American citizen would be as insecure as that of a Frenchman. Ex-Vice-President Dallas tells us that the constitution is an object to which no American mind can be too attentive, and no American heart too devoted. He further says, the constitution, in its words, is plain and intelligible, and is meant for the home-bred, unsophisticated understandings of our fellow-citizens. Senator Berrien tell us that the Constitution is the fundamental law, that which controls all others. The charter of our liberties, which every citizen has a personal interest in understanding thoroughly. The testimony of Senator Breese, Lewis Cass, and many others that might be named, who are everywhere esteemed as sound lawyers, so regard the constitution. I take it, therefore, that it is not presumption in a private citizen to form an opinion of that instrument.

Now, take the constitution according to its plain reading, and I defy the presentation of a single pro-slavery clause in it. On the other hand it will be found to contain principles and purposes, entirely hostile to the existence of slavery.

I have detained my audience entirely too long already. At some future period I will gladly avail myself of an opportunity to give this subject a full and fair discussion. Allow me to say, in conclusion, notwithstanding the dark picture I have this day presented of the state of the nation, I do not despair of this country."

Allow me to say, in conclusion, notwithstanding the dark picture I have this day presented of the state of the nation, I do not despair of this country. There are forces in operation, which must inevitably work the downfall of slavery. "The arm of the Lord is not shortened," and the doom of slavery is certain. I, therefore, leave off where I began, with hope. While drawing encouragement from the Declaration of Independence, the great principles it contains, and the genius of American Institutions, my spirit is also cheered by the obvious tendencies of the age. Nations do not now stand in the same relation to each other that they did ages ago. No nation can now shut itself up from the surrounding world, and trot round in the same old path of its fathers without interference. The time was when such could be done. Long established customs of hurtful character could formerly fence themselves in, and do their evil work with social impunity. Knowledge was then confined and enjoyed by the privileged few, and the multitude walked on in mental darkness. But a change has now come over the affairs of mankind. Walled cities and empires have become unfashionable. The arm of commerce has borne away the gates of the strong city. Intelligence is penetrating the darkest corners of the globe. It makes its pathway over and under the sea, as well as on the earth. Wind, steam, and lightning are its chartered agents. Oceans no longer divide, but link nations together. From Boston to London is now a holiday excursion. Space is comparatively annihilated. Thoughts expressed on one side of the Atlantic are, distinctly heard on the other.

The far-off and almost fabulous Pacific rolls in grandeur at our feet. The Celestial Empire, the mystery of ages, is being solved. The fiat of the Almighty, "Let there be Light," has not yet spent its force. No abuse, no outrage whether in taste, sport or avarice, can now hide itself from the all-pervading light. The iron shoe, and crippled foot of China must be seen, in contrast with nature. Africa must rise and put on her yet unwoven garment. "Ethiopia shall stretch out her hand unto God." In the fervent aspirations of William Lloyd Garrison, I say, and let every heart join in saying it:

God speed the year of jubilee The wide world o'er When from
their galling chains set free, Th' oppress'd shall vilely bend the
knee, And wear the yoke of tyranny Like brutes no more. That
year will come, and freedom's reign, To man his plundered
fights again Restore.

God speed the day when human blood Shall cease to flow! In
every crime be understood, The claims of human brotherhood,
And each return for evil, good, Not blow for blow; That day will
come all feuds to end. And change into a faithful friend Each
foe.

God speed the hour, the glorious hour, When none on earth
Shall exercise a lordly power, Nor in a tyrant's presence cower;
But all to manhood's stature tower, By equal birth! That hour
will come, to each, to all, And from his prison-house, the thrall
Go forth.

Until that year, day, hour, arrive, With head, and heart, and
hand I'll strive, To break the rod, and rend the give, The spoiler
of his prey deprive- So witness Heaven! And never from my
chosen post, Whatever the peril or the cost, Be driven.

CONSTITUTION OF THE AFRICAN CIVILIZATION SOCIETY
1858

An exclusive black organization that wanted emigration to Liberia in the 1850s. After the war, their initiative changed to help former slaves in the south.

Preamble:

It has pleased Almighty God to permit the interior of Africa to be made known to us during the last few years, by the efforts of missionaries and explorers, to an extent hitherto deemed almost impossible. The facts which have become public concerning its climate, soil, productions, minerals, and vast capabilities for improvements, are such, that we can no longer mistake the intention of the Divine Mind towards Africa. It is evident that the prophecy that "Ethiopia shall soon stretch out her hands unto God", is on the point of fulfillment, and that the work, when commenced, shall be "soon" accomplished, when compared with the apparently slow progress of the Gospel in the other grand divisions of the globe. In order, therefore, to aid in this great work, and promote the civilization and Christianization of Africa, as well as the welfare of her children in all lands, we have formed ourselves into an Association, to be known as the African Civilization Society, and we severally agree to be governed by the following:

CONSTITUTION

Article I
The Society shall be called the "African Civilization Society", and shall act in harmony with all other societies, whose objects are similar to those of this Association.

Article II
The object of this Society shall be the civilization and Christianization of Africa, and of the descendants of African ancestors in any portion of the earth, wherever dispersed. Also, the destruction of the African Slave-trade, by the introduction of lawful commerce and trade into Africa: the promotion of the growth of cotton and other products there, whereby the natives may become industrious producers as well as consumers of articles of commerce: and generally, the elevation of the condition of the colored population of our own country, and of other lands.

Article III
No one shall be sent out under the auspices of this Society, either as a religious teacher, agent, or settler, who shall uphold doctrines which shall justify or aid in perpetuating any system of slavery or involuntary servitude.

Article IV
The donation or subscription of not less than one dollar annually, shall constitute any individual of good moral character a member of this Society; and the payment at one time of twenty-five dollars shall make any person a life-member.

Article V
The officers of this Society shall be a President, Vice-President, a board of twenty Directors, a Recording Secretary, a Corresponding Secretary, and a Treasurer, who shall hold office for one year, and until their successors are regularly chosen.

Article VI
The members of this Society may be distinguished as either active, corresponding, or honorary members.

Article VII
The President shall preside at all meetings of the Society, and in the event of his absence, one of the Vice-Presidents shall discharge his duties.

The Recording Secretary shall keep a regular and distinct account of the transactions of the Society.

The Corresponding Secretary shall conduct the correspondence of the Society, and also act as its General Agent, under the direction, and with the consent of the Board of Directors.

The Treasurer shall keep the accounts, and have charge of the funds of the Society, holding them subject to the control of the Board of Directors.

The Board of Directors shall manage and regulate the affairs of the Society, and shall have power to make bye-laws for its own government, so as to fully control the business and funds of the Society.

Five members of the Board of Directors, when regularly convened, shall constitute a quorum for the transaction of business.

Article VIII
The President, Vice-Presidents, Secretaries, and Treasurer shall be ex-officio members and officers of the Board of Directors.

The Board of Directors shall manage and regulate the affairs of the Society, and shall have power to make bye-laws for its own government, so as to fully control the business and funds of the Society.

Five members of the Board of Directors, when regularly convened, shall constitute a quorum for the transaction of business.

Article IX
The Board of Directors shall have power to form special committees from among their own number, and to fill any vacancy occurring among the officers, for any time intervening before the regular election.

Article X
The Society shall hold an annual meeting during the month of May, on any day the Board of Directors may designate, to elect officers, receive reports, and transact its official business, not otherwise delegated to the Board of Directors.
Special meetings may be held at other times, as the Board of Directors may designate.

Article XI
The Annual Meeting shall consist of the regular officers and members of the Society at the time of such meeting, and of delegates from other cooperating Societies, each Society being entitled to one representative.

Article XII

The Constitution shall be altered only at an annual meeting of the Society, by vote of two thirds of the members present, upon a proposal to that effect transmitted to the Corresponding Secretary, and published in the City of New York, at least two months prior to the annual meeting.

SUPPLEMENT TO THE CONSTITUTION OF THE AFRICAN CIVILIZATION SOCIETY

In order the better to make the origin and objects of the African Civilization Society known, and to define its designs, intentions, and true position, and to secure that harmony and co-operation originally designed with other similar institutions previously established by the colored people of the United States and Canada, as well as that by the friends of the African race in Great Britain, to aid these movements,

Resolved, That the succeeding articles be added as an essential and fundamental part of the Constitution:

Art. 1. The Society is not designed to encourage general emigration, but will aid only such persons as may be practically qualified and suited to promote the development of Christianity, morality, education, mechanical arts, agriculture, commerce, and general improvement; who must always be carefully selected and well recommended, that the progress of civilization may not be obstructed.

Art. 2. The basis of the Society, and ulterior objects in encouraging emigration, shall be—Self-Reliance and Self-Government on the principle of an African Nationality, the African race being the ruling element of the nation, controlling and directing their own affairs.

The First Confiscation Act

This act was passed in 1861 and legalized the seizure of Confederate property, including slaves.

CHAP. LX.–An Act to confiscate Property used for Insurrectionary Purposes.

Be it enacted by the Senate and House of Representatives of the United States of America in Congress assembled, That if, during the present or any future insurrection against the Government of the United States, after the President of the United States shall have declared, by proclamation, that the laws of the United States are opposed, and the execution thereof obstructed, by combinations too powerful to be suppressed by the ordinary course of judicial proceedings, or by the power vested in the marshals by law, any person or persons, his, her, or their agent, attorney, or employé, shall purchase or acquire, sell or give, any property of whatsoever kind or description, with intent to use or employ the same, or suffer the same to be used or employed, in aiding, abetting, or promoting such insurrection or resistance to the laws, or any person or persons engaged therein; or if any person or persons, being the owner or owners of any such property, shall knowingly use or employ, or consent to the use or employment of the same as aforesaid, all such property is hereby declared to be lawful subject of prize and capture wherever found; and it shall be the duty of the President of the United States to cause the same to be seized, confiscated, and condemned.

SEC. 2. And be it further enacted, That such prizes and capture shall be condemned in the district or circuit court of the United States having jurisdiction of the amount, or in admiralty in any district in which the same may be seized, or into which they may be taken and proceedings first instituted.

SEC. 3. And be it further enacted, That the Attorney-General, or any district attorney of the United States in which said property may at the time be, may institute the proceedings of condemnation, and in such case they shall be wholly for the benefit of the United States; or any person may file an information with such attorney, in which case the proceedings shall be for the use of such informer and the United States in equal parts.

SEC. 4. And be it further enacted, That whenever hereafter, during the present insurrection against the Government of the United States, any person claimed to be held to labor or service under the law of any State, shall be required or permitted by the person to whom such labor or service is claimed to be due, or by the lawful agent of such person, to take up arms against the United States, or shall be required or permitted by the person to whom such labor or service is claimed to be due, or his lawful agent, to work or to be employed in or upon any fort, navy yard, dock, armory, ship, entrenchment, or in any military or naval service whatsoever, against the Government and lawful authority of the United States, then, and in every such case, the person to whom such labor or service is claimed to be due shall forfeit his claim to such labor, any law of the State or of the United States to the contrary notwithstanding. And whenever thereafter the person claiming such labor or service shall seek to enforce his claim, it shall be a full and sufficient answer to such claim that the person whose service or labor is claimed had been employed in hostile service against the Government of the United States, contrary to the provisions of this act.

APPROVED, August 6, 1861.

U.S., Statutes at Large, Treaties, and Proclamations of the United States of America, vol. 12 (Boston, 1863), p. 319.

THE EMANCIPATION PROCLAMATION
Jan. 1, 1863

More of a war time strategy than a proclamation of morality, it freed the slaves in the southern states that had seceded, but not in the border states. The Emancipation Proclamation changed the basis for the war, from keeping the Union whole, to the freeing of slaves. Abraham Lincoln believed this to be his tour de force of the war.

"That on the first day of January, in the year of our Lord one thousand eight hundred and sixty-three, all persons held as slaves within any State or designated part of a State, the people whereof shall then be in rebellion against the United States, shall be then, thenceforward, and forever free; and the Executive Government of the United States, including the military and naval authority thereof, will recognize and maintain the freedom of such persons, and will do no act or acts to repress such persons, or any of them, in any efforts they may make for their actual freedom.

"That the Executive will, on the first day of January aforesaid, by proclamation, designate the States and parts of States, if any, in which the people thereof, respectively, shall then be in rebellion against the United States; and the fact that any State, or the people thereof, shall on that day be, in good faith, represented in the Congress of the United States by members chosen thereto at elections wherein a majority of the qualified voters of such State shall have participated, shall, in the absence of strong countervailing testimony, be deemed conclusive evidence that such State, and the people thereof, are not then in rebellion against the United States."

Now, therefore I, Abraham Lincoln, President of the United States, by virtue of the power in me vested as Commander-in-Chief, of the Army and Navy of the United States in time of actual armed rebellion against the authority and government of the United States, and as a fit and necessary war measure for suppressing said rebellion, do, on this first day of January, in the year of our Lord one thousand eight hundred and sixty-three, and in accordance with my purpose so to do publicly proclaimed for the full period of one hundred days, from the day first above mentioned, order and designate as the States and parts of States wherein the people thereof respectively, are this day in rebellion against the United States, the following, to wit:

Arkansas, Texas, Louisiana, (except the Parishes of St. Bernard, Plaquemines, Jefferson, St. John, St. Charles, St. James Ascension, Assumption, Terrebonne, Lafourche, St. Mary, St. Martin, and Orleans, including the City of New Orleans) Mississippi, Alabama, Florida, Georgia, South Carolina, North Carolina, and Virginia, (except the forty-eight counties designated as West Virginia, and also the counties of Berkley, Accomac, Northampton, Elizabeth City, York, Princess Ann, and Norfolk, including the cities of Norfolk and Portsmouth[)], and which excepted parts, are for the present, left precisely as if this proclamation were not issued.

And by virtue of the power, and for the purpose aforesaid, I do order and declare that all persons held as slaves within said designated States, and parts of States, are, and henceforward shall be free; and that the Executive government of the United States, including the military and naval authorities thereof, will recognize and maintain the freedom of said persons.

And I hereby enjoin upon the people so declared to be free to abstain from all violence, unless in necessary self-defence; and I recommend to them that, in all cases when allowed, they labor faithfully for reasonable wages.

And I further declare and make known, that such persons of suitable condition, will be received into the armed service of the United States to garrison forts, positions, stations, and other places, and to man vessels of all sorts in said service.

And upon this act, sincerely believed to be an act of justice, warranted by the Constitution, upon military necessity, I invoke the considerate judgment of mankind, and the gracious favor of Almighty God.

In witness whereof, I have hereunto set my hand and caused the seal of the United States to be affixed.

Done at the City of Washington, this first day of January, in the year of our Lord one thousand eight hundred and sixty three, and of the Independence of the United States of America the eighty-seventh.

By the President: Abraham Lincoln
William H. Seward, Secretary of State.

CHEROKEE EMANCIPATION PROCLAMATION
In effect -June 25, 1863

The Cherokee were divided during the Civil War, with pro-Union and pro Confederate factions. The pro-Union faction issued their own emancipation proclamation following Lincoln's, and went into effect in June of 1863. Most slaves were held by pro-Confederates and few were actually freed.

An Act Providing for the Abolition of Slavery in the Cherokee Nation,

Be it enacted by the Natl Council, That in view of the difficulties and evils which have arisen from the Institution of Slavery and which seem inseperable from its existence in the Cherokee Nation, The Delegation appointed to proceed to Washington are impowered and instructed to assure the President of the U States of the desire of the Authorities and People to remove that Institution from the statures and Soil of the Cherokee Nation and of their wish to provide for that object at once upon the Principle of Compensation to the owners of Slaves not disloyal to the Government of the United States as tendered by Congress to States which shall abolish Slavery to their midst; And in case the Government of the United States accede to this propersition, The Said Delegation are hereby Authorized and instructed to enter into an agreement with the Government for the immediate emancipation of all Slaves in the Cherokee Nation and African Slavery shall therefore be abolished and forever cease to exist in said Nation – and therefore it shall be unlawful for any person to hold a Slave within the limits of the Cherokee Nation. And any person who before any of the Courts of the Nation having jurisdiction in the case shall be found guilty of Holding a Slave or Slaves, Shall be fined in a Sum not less than One thousand Dollars __ nor more than Five thousand Dollars. And any Slave So held in Bondage shall be forever free.
So it __, Enacted

That it Shall be the duty of all the Solicitors throughout this Nation to see that this law is strictly enforced within the limits of their respective Districts. And in case any Solicitor shall fail in the performance of his duty in any such case it shall be compelent for Any Citizen to prosecute the case before this proper Court and see that the law is enforced.

And the Solicitor So failing to perform his duty Shall be punished as provided by law in other cases of Similar delinquency. And all Acts and parts of Acts which may Conflict with the above acts, are hereby repealed.

Cowskin Prairie Lewis Downing, Prest
Feby 18th 1863 Nat Committee
pro tem

Concurred in Council
With the following Amendment Commencing in the 1st page 26th line after the word (Dollars) And all fines arising from this Act shall be put in the Natil Treasury.

Spring Frog Spkr
N Council
Con by Committee Feb 19th 1863
Lewis Downing, Prest
Comtee pro tem

Confederate General Patrick Cleburne's Letter Proposing Freedom and Arming of Slaves
Jan. 2, 1864

*Cleburne writes to General Johnston, with the signature of several other officers, describing the need to free and arm the slaves. He believed that southern independence was more important than the institution of slavery. His many valid points were met with suspicion and hostility, with some generals accusing Cleburne of abolitionist sentiments. Confederate President Davis denounced the proposal, as did the majority of his cabinet..*Commanding General, The Corps, Division, Brigade, and Regimental Commanders of the Army of Tennessee General: Moved by the exigency in which our country is now placed we take the liberty of laying before you, unofficially, our views on the present state of affairs. The subject is so grave, and our views so new, we feel it a duty both to you and the cause that before going further we should submit them for your judgment and receive your suggestions in regard to them. We therefore respectfully ask you to give us an expression of your views in the premises. We have now been fighting for nearly three years, have spilled much of our best blood, and lost, consumed, or thrown to the flames an amount of property equal in value to the specie currency of the world. Through some lack in our system the fruits of our struggles and sacrifices have invariably slipped away from us and left us nothing but long lists of dead and mangled. Instead of standing defiantly on the borders of our territory or harassing those of the enemy, we are hemmed in to-day into less than two-thirds of it, and still the enemy menacingly confronts us at every point with superior forces. Our soldiers can see no end to this state of affairs except in our own exhaustion; hence, instead of rising to the occasion, they are sinking into a fatal apathy, growing weary of hardships and slaughters which promise no results. In this state of things it is easy to understand why there is a growing belief that some black catastrophe is not far ahead of us, and that unless some extraordinary change is soon made in our condition we must overtake it. The consequences of this condition are showing themselves more plainly every day; restlessness of morals spreading everywhere, manifesting itself in the army in a growing disregard for private rights; desertion spreading to a class of soldiers it never dared to tamper with before; military commissions sinking in the estimation of the soldier; our supplies failing; our firesides in ruins. If this state continues much longer we must be subjugated. Every man should endeavor to understand the meaning of subjugation before it is too late. We can give but a faint idea when we say it means the loss of all we now hold most sacred — slaves and all other personal property, lands, homesteads, liberty, justice, safety, pride, manhood. It means that the history of this heroic struggle will be written by the enemy; that our youth will be trained by Northern school teachers; will learn from Northern school books their version of the war; will be impressed by all the influences of history and education to regard our gallant dead as traitors, our maimed veterans as fit objects for derision. It means the crushing of Southern manhood, the hatred of our former slaves, who will, on a spy system, be our secret police. The conqueror's policy is to divide the conquered into factions and stir up animosity among them, and in training an army of negroes the North no doubt holds this thought in perspective. We can see three great causes operating to destroy us: First, the inferiority of our armies to those of the enemy in point of numbers; second, the poverty of our single source of supply in comparison with his several sources; third, the fact that slavery, from being one of our chief sources of strength at the commencement of the war, has now become, in a military point of view, one of our chief sources of weakness.

The enemy already opposes us at every point with superior numbers, and is endeavoring to make the preponderance irresistible. President Davis, in his recent message, says the enemy "has recently ordered a large conscription and made a subsequent call for volunteers, to be followed, if ineffectual by a still further draft." In addition, the President of the United States announces that "he has already in training an army of 100,000 negroes as good as any troops," and every fresh raid he makes and new slice of territory he wrests from us will add to this force. Every soldier in our army already knows and feels our numerical inferiority to the enemy. Want of men in the field has prevented him from reaping the fruits of his victories, and has prevented him from having the furlough he expected after the last reorganization, and when he turns from the wasting armies in the field to look at the source of supply, he finds nothing in the prospect to encourage him. Our single source of supply is that portion of our white men fit for duty and not now in the ranks. The enemy has three sources of supply: First, his own motley population; secondly, our slaves; and thirdly, Europeans whose hearts are fired into a crusade against us by fictitious pictures of the atrocities of slavery, and who meet no hindrance from their Governments in such enterprise, because these Governments are equally antagonistic to the institution. In touching the third cause, the fact that slavery has become a military weakness, we may rouse prejudice and passion, but the time has come when it would be madness not to look at our danger from every point of view, and to probe it to the bottom. Apart from the assistance that home and foreign prejudice against slavery has given to the North, slavery is a source of great strength to the enemy in a purely military point of view, by supplying him with an army from our granaries; but it is our most vulnerable point, a continued embarrassment, and in some respects an insidious weakness. Wherever slavery is once seriously disturbed, whether by the actual presence or the approach of the enemy, or even by a cavalry raid, the whites can no longer with safety to their property openly sympathize with our cause. The fear of their slaves is continually haunting them, and from silence and apprehension many of these soon learn to wish the war stopped on any terms. The next stage is to take the oath to save property, and they become dead to us, if not open enemies. To prevent raids we are forced to scatter our forces, and are not free to move and strike like the enemy; his vulnerable points are carefully selected and fortified depots. Ours are found in every point where there is a slave to set free. All along the lines slavery is comparatively valueless to us for labor, but of great and increasing worth to the enemy for information. It is an omnipresent spy system, pointing out our valuable men to the enemy, revealing our positions, purposes, and resources, and yet acting so safely and secretly that there is no means to guard against it. Even in the heart of our country, where our hold upon this secret espionage is firmest, it waits but the opening fire of the enemy's battle line to wake it, like a torpid serpent, into venomous activity.

In view of the state of affairs what does our country propose to do? In the words of President Davis "no effort must be spared to add largely to our effective force as promptly as possible. The sources of supply are to be found in restoring to the army all who are improperly absent, putting an end to substitution, modifying the exemption law, restricting details, and placing in the ranks such of the able-bodied men now employed as wagoners, nurses, cooks, and other employe[e]s, as are doing service for which the negroes may be found competent." Most of the men improperly absent, together with many of the exempts and men having substitutes, are now without the Confederate lines and cannot be calculated on. If all the exempts capable of bearing arms were enrolled, it will give us the boys below eighteen, the men above forty-five, and those persons who are left at home to meet the wants of the country and the army, but this modification of the exemption law will remove from the fields and manufactories most of the skill that directed agricultural and mechanical labor, and, as stated by the President, "details will have to be made to meet the wants of the country," thus sending many of the men to be derived from this source back to their homes again. Independently of this, experience proves that striplings and men above conscript age break down and swell the sick lists more than they do the ranks. The portion now in our lines of the class who have substitutes is not on the whole a hopeful element, for the motives that created it must have been stronger than patriotism, and these motives added to what many of them will call breach of faith, will cause some to be not forthcoming, and others to be unwilling and discontented soldiers. The remaining sources mentioned by the President have been so closely pruned in the Army of Tennessee that they will be found not to yield largely. The supply from all these sources, together with what we now have in the field, will exhaust the white race, and though it should greatly exceed expectations and put us on an equality with the enemy, or even give us temporary advantages, still we have no reserve to meet unexpected disaster or to supply a protracted struggle. Like past years, 1864 will diminish our ranks by the casualties of war, and what source of repair is there left us? We therefore see in the recommendations of the President only a temporary expedient, which at the best will leave us twelve months hence in the same predicament we are in now. The President attempts to meet only one of the depressing causes mentioned; for the other two he has proposed no remedy. They remain to generate lack of confidence in our final success, and to keep us moving down hill as heretofore. Adequately to meet the-causes which are now threatening ruin to our country, we propose, in addition to a modification of the President's plans, that we retain in service for the war all troops now in service, and that we immediately commence training a large reserve of the most courageous of our slaves, and further that we guarantee freedom within a reasonable time to every slave in the South who shall remain true to the Confederacy in this war. As between the loss of independence and the loss of slavery, we assume that every patriot will freely give up the latter — give up the negro slave rather than be a slave himself. If we are correct in this assumption it only remains to show how this great national sacrifice is, in all human probabilities, to change the current of success and sweep the invader from our country.

Our country has already some friends in England and France, and there are strong motives to induce these nations to recognize and assist us, but they cannot assist us without helping slavery, and to do this would be in conflict with their policy for the last quarter of a century. England has paid hundreds of millions to emancipate her West India slaves and break up the slave-trade. Could she now consistently spend her treasure to reinstate slavery in this country? But this barrier once removed, the sympathy and the interests of these and other nations will accord with our own, and we may expect from them both moral support and material aid. One thing is certain, as soon as the great sacrifice to independence is made and known in foreign countries there will be a complete change of front in our favor of the sympathies of the world. This measure will deprive the North of the moral and material aid which it now derives from the bitter prejudices with which foreigners view the institution, and its war, if continued, will henceforth be so despicable in their eyes that the source of recruiting will be dried up. It will leave the enemy's negro army no motive to fight for, and will exhaust the source from which it has been recruited. The idea that it is their special mission to war against slavery has held growing sway over the Northern people for many years, and has at length ripened into an armed and bloody crusade against it. This baleful superstition has so far supplied them with a courage and constancy not their own. It is the most powerful and honestly entertained plank in their war platform. Knock this away and what is left? A bloody ambition for more territory, a pretended veneration for the Union, which one of their own most distinguished orators (Doctor Beecher in his Liverpool speech) openly avowed was only used as a stimulus to stir up the anti-slavery crusade, and lastly the poisonous and selfish interests which are the fungus growth of the war itself. Mankind may fancy it a great duty to destroy slavery, but what interest can mankind have in upholding this remainder of the Northern war platform? Their interests and feelings will be diametrically opposed to it. The measure we propose will strike dead all John Brown fanaticism, and will compel the enemy to draw off altogether or in the eyes of the world to swallow the Declaration of Independence without the sauce and disguise of philanthropy. This delusion of fanaticism at an end, thousands of Northern people will have leisure to look at home and to see the gulf of despotism into which they themselves are rushing. The measure will at one blow strip the enemy of foreign sympathy and assistance, and transfer them to the South; it will dry up two of his three sources of recruiting; it will take from his negro army the only motive it could have to fight against the South, and will probably cause much of it to desert over to us; it will deprive his cause of the powerful stimulus of fanaticism, and will enable him to see the rock on which his so-called friends are now piloting him. The immediate effect of the emancipation and enrollment of negroes on the military strength of the South would be: To enable us to have armies numerically superior to those of the North, and a reserve of any size we might think necessary; to enable us to take the offensive, move forward, and forage on the enemy. It would open to us in prospective another and almost untouched source of supply, and furnish us with the means of preventing temporary disaster, and carrying on a protracted struggle. It would instantly remove all the vulnerability, embarrassment, and inherent weakness which result from slavery. The approach of the enemy would no longer find every household surrounded by spies; the fear that sealed the master's lips and the avarice that has, in so many cases, tempted him practically to desert us would alike be removed. There would be no recruits awaiting the enemy with open arms, no complete history of every neighborhood with ready guides, no fear of insurrection in the rear, or anxieties for the fate of loved ones when our armies moved forward. The chronic irritation of hope deferred would be joyfully ended with the negro, and the sympathies of his whole race would be due to his native South. It would restore confidence in an early termination of the war with all its inspiring consequences, and even if contrary to all expectations the enemy should succeed in over-running the South, instead of finding a cheap, ready-made means of holding it down, he would find a common hatred and thirst for vengeance, which would break into acts at every favorable opportunity, would prevent him from settling on our lands, and render the South a very unprofitable conquest. It would remove forever all selfish taint from our cause and place independence above every question of property. The very magnitude of the sacrifice itself, such as no nation has ever voluntarily made before, would appal [sic] our enemies, destroy his spirit and his finances, and fill our hearts with a pride and singleness of purpose which would clothe us with new strength in battle. Apart from all other aspects of the question, the necessity for more fighting men is upon us. We can only get a sufficiency by making the negro share the danger and hardships of the war. If we arm and train him and make him fight for the country in her hour of dire distress, every consideration of principle and policy demand that we should set him and his whole race who side with us free. It is a first principle with mankind that he who offers his life in defense of the State should receive from her in return his freedom and his happiness, and we believe in acknowledgment of this principle. The Constitution of the Southern States has reserved to their respective governments the power to free slaves for meritorious services to the State. It is politic besides. For many years, ever since the agitation of the subject of slavery commenced, the negro has been dreaming of freedom, and his vivid imagination has surrounded that condition with so many gratifications that it has become the paradise of his hopes. To attain it he will tempt dangers and difficulties not exceeded by the bravest soldier in the field. The hope of freedom is perhaps the only moral incentive that can be applied to him in his present condition. It would be preposterous then to expect him to fight against it with any degree of enthusiasm, therefore we must bind him to our cause by no doubtful bonds; we must leave no possible loop-hole for treachery to creep in. The slaves are dangerous now, but armed, trained, and collected in an army they would be a thousand fold more dangerous; therefore when we make soldiers of them we must make free men of them beyond all question, and thus enlist their sympathies also. We can do this more effectually than the North can now do, for we can give the negro not only his own freedom, but that of his wife and child, and can secure it to him in his old home. To do this, we must immediately make his marriage and parental relations sacred in the eyes of the law and forbid their sale. The past legislation of the South concedes that a large free middle class of negro blood, between the master and slave, must sooner or later destroy the institution. If, then, we touch the institution at all, we would do best to make the most of it, and by emancipating the whole race upon reasonable terms, and within such reasonable time as will prepare both races for the change, secure to ourselves all the advantages, and to our enemies all the disadvantages that can arise, both at home and abroad, from such a sacrifice. Satisfy the negro that if he faithfully adheres to our standard during the war he shall receive his freedom and that of his race. Give him as an earnest of our intentions such immediate immunities as will impress him with our sincerity and be in keeping with his new condition, enroll a portion of his class as soldiers of the Confederacy, and we change the race from a dreaded weakness to a position of strength. Will the slaves fight? The helots of Sparta stood their masters good stead in battle. In the great sea fight of Lepanto where the Christians checked forever the spread of Mohammedanism over Europe, the galley slaves of portions of the fleet were promised freedom, and called on to fight at a critical moment of the battle. They fought well, and civilization owes much to those brave galley slaves. The negro slaves of Saint Domingo, fighting for freedom, defeated their white masters and the French troops sent against them. The negro slaves of Jamaica revolted, and under the name of Maroons held the mountains against their masters for 150 years; and the experience of this war has been so far that half-trained negroes have fought as bravely as many other half-trained Yankees. If, contrary to the training of a lifetime, they can be made to face and fight bravely against their former masters, how much more probable is it that with the allurement of a higher reward, and led by those masters, they would submit to discipline and face dangers.

We will briefly notice a few arguments against this course. It is said Republicanism cannot exist without the institution. Even were this true, we prefer any form of government of which the Southern people may have the molding, to one forced upon us by a conqueror. It is said the white man cannot perform agricultural labor in the South. The experience of this army during the heat of summer from Bowling Green, Ky., to Tupelo, Miss., is that the white man is healthier when doing reasonable work in the open field than at any other time. It is said an army of negroes cannot be spared from the fields. A sufficient number of slaves is now administering to luxury alone to supply the place of all we need, and we believe it would be better to take half the able-bodied men off a plantation than to take the one master mind that economically regulated its operations. Leave some of the skill at home and take some of the muscle to fight with. It is said slaves will not work after they are freed. We think necessity and a wise legislation will compel them to labor for a living. It is said it will cause terrible excitement and some disaffection from our cause. Excitement is far preferable to the apathy which now exists, and disaffection will not be among the fighting men. It is said slavery is all we are fighting for, and if we give it up we give up all. Even if this were true, which we deny, slavery is not all our enemies are fighting for. It is merely the pretense to establish sectional superiority and a more centralized form of government, and to deprive us of our rights and liberties. We have now briefly proposed a plan which we believe will save our country. It may be imperfect, but in all human probability it would give us our independence. No objection ought to outweigh it which is not weightier than independence. If it is worthy of being put in practice it ought to be mooted quickly before the people, and urged earnestly by every man who believes in its efficacy. Negroes will require much training; training will require much time, and there is danger that this concession to common sense may come too late.

P. R. Cleburne, major-general, commanding division
D. C. Govan, brigadier-general
John E. Murray, colonel, Fifth Arkansas
G. F. Baucum, colonel, Eighth Arkansas
Peter Snyder, lieutenant-colonel, commanding Sixth and Seventh Arkansas
E. Warfield, lieutenant-colonel, Second Arkansas
M. P. Lowrey, brigadier-general
A. B. Hardcastle, colonel, Thirty-second and Forty-fifth Mississippi
F. A. Ashford, major, Sixteenth Alabama
John W. Colquitt, colonel, First Arkansas
Rich. J. Person, major, Third and Fifth Confederate
G. S. Deakins, major, Thirty-fifth and Eighth Tennessee
J. H. Collett, captain, commanding Seventh Texas
J. H. Kelly, brigadier-general, commanding Cavalry Division

General William T. Sherman's Special Field Order NO. 15
Jan. 16, 1865

Sherman confiscated about 400,000 acres of land in South Carolina, Georgia and Florida and divided it into small parcels for former slaves and their families to live. These parcels were 40 acres and it is where the "Forty acres and a mule" idea comes from, even though mules are not mentioned here, Sherman gave another order for mules to be sent to the confiscated area. President Johnson, reversed this order.

I. The islands from Charleston, south, the abandoned rice fields along the rivers for thirty miles back from the sea, and the country bordering the St. Johns River, Florida, are reserved and set apart for the settlement of the negroes now made free by the acts of war and the proclamation of the President of the United States.

II. At Beaufort, Hilton Head, Savannah, Fernandina, St. Augustine and Jacksonville, the blacks may remain in their chosen or accustomed vocations—but on the islands, and in the settlements hereafter to be established, no white person whatever, unless military officers and soldiers detailed for duty, will be permitted to reside; and the sole and exclusive management of affairs will be left to the freed people themselves, subject only to the United States military authority and the acts of Congress. By the laws of war, and orders of the President of the United States, the negro is free and must be dealt with as such. He cannot be subjected to conscription or forced military service, save by the written orders of the highest military authority of the Department, under such regulations as the President or Congress may prescribe. Domestic servants, blacksmiths, carpenters and other mechanics, will be free to select their own work and residence, but the young and able-bodied negroes must be encouraged to enlist as soldiers in the service of the United States, to contribute their share towards maintaining their own freedom, and securing their rights as citizens of the United States.

Negroes so enlisted will be organized into companies, battalions and regiments, under the orders of the United States military authorities, and will be paid, fed and clothed according to law. The bounties paid on enlistment may, with the consent of the recruit, go to assist his family and settlement in procuring agricultural implements, seed, tools, boots, clothing, and other articles necessary for their livelihood.

Map Showing 400,000 acres (in Orange) Granted to 10,000 Freedpeople in January 1865

III. Whenever three respectable negroes, heads of families, shall desire to settle on land, and shall have selected for that purpose an island or a locality clearly defined, within the limits above designated, the Inspector of Settlements and Plantations will himself, or by such subordinate officer as he may appoint, give them a license to settle such island or district, and afford them such assistance as he can to enable them to establish a peaceable agricultural settlement. The three parties named will subdivide the land, under the supervision of the Inspector, among themselves and such others as may choose to settle near them, so that each family shall have a plot of not more than (40) forty acres of tillable ground, and when it borders on some water channel, with not more than 800 feet water front, in the possession of which land the military authorities will afford them protection, until such time as they can protect themselves, or until Congress shall regulate their title. The Quartermaster may, on the requisition of the Inspector of Settlements and Plantations, place at the disposal of the Inspector, one or more of the captured steamers, to ply between the settlements and one or more of the commercial points heretofore named in orders, to afford the settlers the opportunity to supply their necessary wants, and to sell the products of their land and labor.

IV. Whenever a negro has enlisted in the military service of the United States, he may locate his family in any one of the settlements at pleasure, and acquire a homestead, and all other rights and privileges of a settler, as though present in person. In like manner, negroes may settle their families and engage on board the gunboats, or in fishing, or in the navigation of the inland waters, without losing any claim to land or other advantages derived from this system. But no one, unless an actual settler as above defined, or unless absent on Government service, will be entitled to claim any right to land or property in any settlement by virtue of these orders.

V. In order to carry out this system of settlement, a general officer will be detailed as Inspector of Settlements and Plantations, whose duty it shall be to visit the settlements, to regulate their police and general management, and who will furnish personally to each head of a family, subject to the approval of the President of the United States, a possessory title in writing, giving as near as possible the description of boundaries; and who shall adjust all claims or conflicts that may arise under the same, subject to the like approval, treating such titles altogether as possessory. The same general officer will also be charged with the enlistment and organization of the negro recruits, and protecting their interests while absent from their settlements; and will be governed by the rules and regulations prescribed by the War Department for such purposes.

VI. Brigadier General R. SAXTON is hereby appointed Inspector of Settlements and Plantations, and will at once enter on the performance of his duties. No change is intended or desired in the settlement now on Beaufort [Port Royal] Island, nor will any rights to property heretofore acquired be affected thereby.

By order of Major General W. T. Sherman:

Constitutional Amendment 13
Dec. 18, 1865

This amendment to the Constitution abolished slavery, except for when punished for a crime in the United States.

Amendment XIII
Passed by Congress January 31, 1865. Ratified December 6, 1865.

Section 1.
Neither slavery nor involuntary servitude, except as a punishment for crime whereof the party shall have been duly convicted, shall exist within the United States, or any place subject to their jurisdiction.

Section 2.
Congress shall have power to enforce this article by appropriate legislation.

Part of the New Deal programs, the Works Progress Administration was initially founded to employ those out of work to build roads, bridges, schools, and parks for the common good of the public. The WPA also employed many in the arts, like the Federal Writers' Project. The FWP interviewed over 2000 former slaves about their lives during bondage. There are fourteen interviews in this collection. The interviews were written down in the African-American vernacular at the time, making some of it difficult to read.

Kate Dudley Baumont.

Ex-slave, age unknown

"I wuz very young when freedom come; still I can member lots of t'tings, en then, too, my fam'ly been in slavery foh sech a long time, dat dey offen talked, en told us so much bout t'tings dat happened."

"I wuz bawned in Bass County, Kentucky, jes' twelve miles from Mt. Sterling. Father en Mother wuz owned by a Mr. Preston of Lexington.

Dey had been give to him when he got married - in fact, his folks give him twenty of us slaves. Mr. Preston lived in Lexington, en had a fine place en sev'ral house servants. Den too, he had de fahm near Mt. Sterling, of bout 200 acres, en twenty of us - or thereabouts - lived on dat place. Dey was five of us childun; Will, Lewis, Lucindie, Harriet en me."

"Our mother died when we wuz very young, en our grandmother looked after us. Grandmother en my aunt Nancy wuz very fine seamstresses, en dey would go in town to de Preston home, en sew for weeks at a time makin' close fod de whole fam'ly. Us childun's close wuz well made en we had much more den some slaves, cause my grandmother en aunt see to it day we had t'ings, en dey made some of de t'ings day made foh de Preston girls. "e did have to go bare-foot in summer time, but when de weather got cool we begun to wear shoes."

Mr. Preston would come out once in a while, en I member him giv-in' us all nickels, en some of de older ones a good little bit of money."

"We had a church bout t'roo miles from us, on a preacher called Uncle Willis, who later wua a school teacher, en we went to school to him." "A lot of men from our place went to war. I had two uncles what went. It wuz nothin' to see sojers in our neighborhood. When de wah wuz ovah, Mr. Preston give all his slaves deeds foh so much land, en built em each a little four-room cottage. Some of dem folks is still on dat piece of land."

"We moved to Lexin'ton aftuh a few yeahs, en latuh to Gawgtown.

I married Mr. Robert Baumont, from Orange County, Vi'ginia, en we went to Cincinnati. We moved from Cincinnati to Springfield bout twenty-five years ago."

"When we lived on de Preston farm somethin happened dat raised a lot of talk. One de Preston girls fell in love with de Negro coachman en run off en married him in Canada. Said she never wanted to marry a white man. She never did have no white beaux as a girl."

"Her father wuz so hurt en he said he wuz goin' to disown her; but he did give em $10,000. Den he said he never wanted them to come back to visit him or his folks, but his folks could go up to Canada en visit with her en her fam'ly."

"Befoh, de Prestons threatened to kill de man, but de girl she said if dey killed him she would kill some of dem en herself, too. She told dem dat she pu'suaded him to take her, en dat she had been in love with him foh years, en had tried ever so long to git him to run off with her en marry her. Ole Miss like to a died, but she got ovah it, en took trips up to Canadada when she wanted to see her daughter. But de girl en her husband dey nevuh come back to her old home."

"Dey had a fam'ly, so we heard, en he wuz doin' well, en had some kind of business, en latuh, it wuz said, he made a lot of money. He wuz a nice lookin' man; dark, but fine featured."

"Preston's slaves wuz same as free in dem times. De ones on his farm, dey tended dey own land en wuz dey own boss. Folks said helet his darkies be free, en some of em talked a lot en said dat when his daugther married."

"I know dey did'ny call a doctor foh evuh little t'ing in de old days, like dey do now; dey used home remedies, en I learned to be a midwife en nurse when I grew up. I cant t'ink of some of de t'ings used in dem days. I know we used ground ivy foh measles, en water melon seed tea to make young babies kidneys act. Cucumber rinds wuz always good to rub on de face to remove freckles, en some people do dat now."

"When we went to church we sung lots of dem good ole hymns, like; "I want Jesus to Walk With Me; Every Day En Ev8ry Hour"; Take my Burdens To De Lord"; en "Bells Done Rung En I'm goin' Home".

"Me en my two daughters is all they is left. I go up to de Penta-costal Church, on South Yellow Springs Street, en both my girls go to de Second Baptist Church."

HENRY BEDFORD
Ex-slave- 78 years old

I wuz eight years ole when de slaves wuz freed, en I mem-ber lots. I wuz bawn en Millersburg, Tennessee. My fam'ly dey belong ter Dr. John Bedford. He had 800 slaves en 1,000 acres of land.

"Dey wuz six of us chillun, Laura, Emma, Alex, Gaston, Pat., en me; en I'se de on'y one left."

"Dr. Bedford wuz good ter all his slaves; he fed em good en clothed em good. Dey wuz so menny cabindat it look like er little town, wid er long dirt road fer de main street. When de fam'lies got bigger, dey jus added on ter de cabins, so de fam'lies ud have nuff room. De mothers of de diffu'nt fam'lies done de cooking fer dey own set of chillun."

"Dey wuz er great big fire place, and us used big logs ter burn en it, en when one dem big logs wuz trowed on de fire it done light up de room fine. De food wuz plent'ful, en us had pork, fresh en cured meat, en wild meat sich as rabbits, possums, en coons. Dey wuz plenty of fish, tu'key en de winter, en all kines veg'tables, en us wuz fed well.

"De big house of Dr. Bedford's wuz real pretty en furnished what you call fine; big high ["fine" crossed out] beds, bookcases, tables en cabinets, en dey had er fine pianny."

"None of us Bedford slaves ebber wuz whipped; he didn' stand fer dat, even fum de patrollers. Ef you say you wuz Dr. Bedford's slave dem ole patrollers diden' touch you."

"Dey wuz er church on de plantation fer de slaves, en er dance hall where dey had dances. De music wuz de fiddle, banjo, en Jewssharp; but mos'ly dey played de fiddle."

"All de cloth en shoes wuz made right dere on de planation. Dr. Bedford had a great big cabin where de 'omans done weave de cloth fer all de close en beddin'. He had er shoe shop where all de shoes wuz made, en believe me, dey wuz some good weavers en cobblers on date place."

"Ben Johnson en Beard had plantations dat jined our'n. Dey wuz both mean as de Ole Nick. I seed em whip slaves till dey mos' daid, en throw em en er ditch dat run through de place. Dr. Bedford he tuk em out en treated em, en jus' kep' em. One 'time, Ben Johnson went to court a-bout it, but he diden' git nowhere. De jedge, he say, 'Well, you think dis slave wuz daid, diden' you? Now he belongs ter Dr. Bedford.' Dat happen lots o' times - him gittin' slaves half daid, en doctorin' em, and den he jus' kep' em."

"I member seein' lots o' de men fun our place goin' off to war, en I heerd em talkin' bout runnin' off ter de Nawth. When de diffu'nt armies come through, I member seein' Grant en Sherman, en ole Giner'l Bragg de rebel gin'rel, en lots more I don't member. But I aint so good at callin' names now."

"I seen big baptizin's. One time I seed 210 baptize en de Tennessee River. Dey sing 'Gimmie De Ole Time Religion', 'Wuz I Bawn Ter Die En Lay Dis Body Down', en lots more.

"When I wuz er kid us played 'Goose en Gander', Hide en Seek', Drop de Hanku'chief, en 'Ring 'round 'Rosie'," I wus married bout forty years ago, In Chat'nooga, Tenn-essee. Us married at de preacher's house, with no big party ner put on.

Us been here en Springfield bout 29 or 30 years. Both us belongs ter St. John Baptist Church."

CHARLES GREEN.
Ex-slave, 78 years

"I wuz bawn in Mason County, Kaintucky, in 1859, en I wuz 78 my last birthday, May 3. Mother en father wuz Mary en Henry Green. Ole

man Wallingsford owned mother, en my two sisters en me; father he be-longed to Charles Dobbins."

"Wallingsford owned a fair size plantation, en he raised rye, wheat, cawn, en cattle en sheep. He allus had bout 1500 sheep."

"Ole Miss wuz good ter us; but him, de devil wuz'nt no meaner."

"Us allus slep' in de kitchen en de winter, but wen de weather got warm nough us slep' out on er porch. Mother wuz de cook, en done all kine er wuk bout de place - washing', iron', weavin', all else what dey tole her ter do. Den she died, en us chilluns wuz left ter de care er Ole Miss. She wuz jus' as sweet - lak er angel."

"I doan guess none er de slaves knowed whut it wuz ter have much clothes, us went bar'foot fum March ter November whilst Ole Marse lived, but Ole Miss wuz heap mo' considahrat; all de same us went bar'foot mos' all er time en good weather."

"Us nebber had no books, en nebber played no games 'cept marbles en mumblin' peg."

"When us went to church us goes ter de white folks church en set en er back seats. Dey wuz Ironside Baptist. Dey uster sing a song called "Come Ter De Ole Church Yard." "When ole John Morgan came through a raidin', he tuk meat en hosses fum ouah place, en jes' lef de smokehouse empty."

"Father en my half-brother George Spencer Green jined up with the 112th Kaintucky boys, en wuz with Gin'ral Sherman marchin' ter de sea. Father he died, but Spence comes home arter de war en settled en er lower paht er Mason County. Us, me en the girls, Martha en Nannie went ter live with George Spencer kaze he wuz my half-brother. I worked roun' on farms, en finely in 1881, I came ter Springfield.

"I built me er shanty on East Main St. jes' below de stan'pipe. All youn' wuz woods. East Street Shops wua just startin' ter be built en I carried de hod fer it en de Arcade, en Metallic Casket, en er Y.M.C.A.; en I mixed all er mortar fer de Fairbanks Building.

'I go t married. My wife en five er my chilluns are daid. I got five chillun livin'."

"Way back in de days when I was a chile, folks tole us chilluns dat ef us wuz bad de witches gwin'ter make de goun' hot whe'evah us walked, en our feet would burn sho'. Dey say de ole devil gwine'ter stick er pitchfork en us ef us wuz bad, en snakes ud crawl en our hair, en lots o' things dat nobody nebber teaches chillun now. But fact is; folks is got lots more reasonin' now den when I come'long."

"Us thought de Yankee soldiers wuz comin' ter carry us off, en dey tole us ter hide if us seen em. I member one night; twuz mos' dark; I seed some Yankee soldiers, en I wuz skeered ter death. Dey yelled at me, en I tuk ter my heels; den dey shot en de air en I run all de faster gittin' back ter de house.   But when Ole John Morgan come along a-raidin' en carryin' off de meat en good hosses us wuz'nt fraid."

"Dey wuz'nt sca'cely no churches fer cullud folks till atter de war; den lots er churches sprung up. Hood many er de preachers could'nt read, but de could take er text en preach er good sermonfum it.

"Rev. George W. Downings, Brother DuPree, Leslie Green, en lotslike em gotter be moughty great preachers."

'I learned to read a little atter de war, en I is moghty glad,kaze since I caint do much, its lots er company ter be able ter read.

JULIA ANN JAMES
Ex-Slave, age 83 years.

"I cum fum Rickin'ham County, Nawth Cah'lina. 'Course I wuz'nt very big when de war broke out, but I can member lots o'things."

"Mother wuz named Cah'lina, en father wuz Cain Smith. Dey both belong ter de same fam'ly but dey live en diffu'nt places. Six us chillun en mother stayed with ole Marse Drewry Smith. He had sech er big fam'ly dat dey done live en all diffu'nt parts en tended things fer him on his other plantations. Smith owned mos' all o' Stokes, Scurry, Forsyth, en Rockin'ham Counties, en he had er thousand slaves. He had 20 chillun- 'leven by his first wife en nine by de second wife.

"Marse Drewry had his own tan yard, right dere on de place, en five stillhouses. Dey wuz shoemakers, harness makers, en weavers what wuk all de time. He done hire sev'ral poor white 'omans what done weavin' fer twenty five cents er day. Three cooks wuk in de kitchen all de time. Some de 'omens dey kep' busy makin' shirts, en dresses fer de girls.

"De Smith boys en girls had plenty o' dey own pusnal slaves. Dey wuz er gang of em, en eight o'de boys wuz en de Rebel armies at one time."

"Mother wuked en de field. I done lots o' knittin'- stockin's en sech like. Many de time I used broom straws fer knitten needles. Us dyed our own cloth fum walnut hulls en wood, brush blossoms, en sometimes copper te help mek er diffu'ny colorin'. Course de color wuz'nt jes'. as pretty as dey mek now, but dat dye it wash good en diden mek de goods fall ter pieces, like some de stuff dey use now

SAMUEL LYONS
Ex-Slave, age unknown

"I wuz mos" er young man when de wah bruk out, but I doan know my 'zact age, kaze de book what had our ages wrote en it got burnt up when Evall's house wuz burnt."

"I wuz bawn en Sawhill Station, Bourbon County, Kaintucky. Julie Ann wuz my mother's name, en my father wuz Sam Lyons, but he died en my mother got married ergin ter Gawge Conley."

"Evall he had erbout 200 slaves en er big plantation en fine race horses. He raised cane, wheat en cawn, en he had er big stillhouse ferter mak he's own whiskey, en he made it ter sell too."

"Us done our cookin' en our cabin, en twuz'nt much 'cept jowl bacon, cawn bread en syrup.

"Me en part of our fam'ly wuz sold onct, en ole Miss Evall's mother brought us back the same day."

"I seen slaves whipped at de whipping post en Baris, Kaintucky, till dey backs bleed, en den dey springle de cuts with salty water."

"Diffunt slave owners take de slaves ter help over slave owners cut dey winter's wood, er husk cawn, er shear dey sheep. Us done got good food den, en sometines dey uster let der slaves have dances togedder, whilst dey wuz wulkin' ter git de wuk done up."

"Evall bought our shoes in Paris, en ef dey wuz too big us wored em,en ef dey wuz too little us wored em jes' de same; but sometimes us cut detoes outer de shoes ter mek em long enough." "When de wah bruk out some de folks fum our plantation went off ter

it. Bout dat time Evall give us our freedom papers, but mother had ter go inter Paris en git de papers her ownself. Us chillun made/out de papers wid him."

"Us went ter Covin'ton, Kaintucky, en wuked en er terbacker fac-tory en done whatever wuk us cud git ter do. I stayed dere fur 'bout six months, en den I moved ter Goes Station en wuked en de powder mills. En after twelve years dere, us moved ter Springfiled."

"I member when all dis west enn er town wuz nothin' but er woods. I Member when all de land betwixt Lowry en Race Streets, fum Fair ter Pleas-ant Street wuz nothin' but er big orchard."

"Folks uster be feard of hoodooin' en being witched. Dey uster carry de bone of a cat leg, flint stones, en dried dogwood blossoms fer good luck. Dey uster take bittersweet en put in en er pan with er little grease, an atter it wuz het pour off de grease en use it fer sa've ter cure rheumatism. Dey uster tek sheep nannie tea for measles, en lots o'things what seems quare now. Now, folks dey doan use sech things like dat."

"I tend Wiley M. E. Church. I'se de on'y one of my fam'ly left. My wife been daid 'bout eight years."

"I uster know Asberry Whiteman well. He's one de early preachers en dis town, en he uster preach at Nawth Street Church.

"If I wuz talkin' te some ole timer like myself lots of things us jes' come back ter me clear like, but I fergit so much now, kaze its been so long ergo."

"I wuz bawned in Bath County, Kentucky, Jan. 17, 1847. My father wuz Bryant McIntire, en my mother wuz Sally McIntire. Father wuz took by slave traders from Africa, en dey done bring him to Norfolk, Virginia,
en put him on de block, en sold him to Jim Lane of Bath County, Kentucky, Lane made de first cookin' stove man'factered en de United States west of New York. It wuz made at Ashland, Kentucky, en it burned wood."

"Lane en de people what owned mother wuz friends, en betwixt em dey give father en mother en order so dey cud be man en wife. You see, in dem days all dey done wuz to giver er order in writin' fer a man er
woman ter be man er wife. Lane wuz a little mo' human den some of de slave owners back in den times, so he 'lowed mother en father to go by de name of McIntire as de married name."

"Dey wuz ten of us chillun: Hannah, Lomie, Melvinie, Sally, Williams, Georgia, Wash, Tannar, John, en me."

"Jim Lane owned 550 slaves en about 2,000 acres of good land. He wuz one of de big rich men in dem days, en I reckon he's be de same now. He had a big, red brick house with 24 rooms, en he needed em, fer he had six-teen shillun, en he wuz allus havin' company en lots of it."

"De slave quarters quz 'bout 300 yards from de big house, en ev'ry fam'ly had dew own cabin en eight acres of land fer dey ownself's, en all de vegetables en garden truck dey needed. Dey raied dey own chickens en tu'keys. But de hogs en cattle wuz butchered en shared with all de diffu'nt fam'lies, en so wuz de milk."
"But I members hearin' my folks talkin', en 'twuz'nt jes' eats dey wanted. Dey wanted ter to be free, en larn dey chillun, like Marse Jim's chillun, so dey cud grow up en have som'thin fer dem selves. I'd offen hear em sayin "Nebber min' chillun, fer yer auntie is sho' a comin'"
Dat wuz jest a blind fer sayin', "Freedom's comin'. Us chillun soon learnt what it meant, but de white folks nebber did learn."

"We had a ladder nex' to de side of de cabin, en us chillun climb up in de lof' en slep' on straw ticks laid on de floot. Manys de time I waked up en foun' snow all on our bed, done sifted t'rough de tracks in de ceilin'."

"Our cloes wuz jeans pants en coarse hickory shirts, en big hard shoes made by de shoemakers on de plantation. De wuz three or four of dem, en day made de harnesses fer de hosses. We had jes' one pair o' shoes a year, en my mother she's sew up moccasins fer us ter protect our feet 'fore time to begin wearin' shoes. Mos' times it wuz near Christmas 'fore shoes wuz wore."

"I never seen a Lane slave whipped ner treated cruel, en he nebber lowed none of hist fam'lies ter be separated. Dat wuz de reason he had so many slaves, kaze when he went to sales he's jes' buy a whole fam'ly fore he'd 'low dem all be sep'rated. Den when his chillun married he'd give em four or five families, but he nebber give no writin' with em. So dey couldnt sell em.

"My grandmother was a weaver, en dey wuz sev'ral other weavers. My mother wuz a cook en a midwife.

"Dey wuz a log church right on our plantation fer us to attend, en other slaves from other plantations come en had meetin's with us. Dey uster sing lots of good ole fashion songs, but I jes' cant think of em right
Now." "Lane en some of his friends had em a little church dey build fer demselfs, en dey allus walk from our plantation kaze he wuz quite 'ligious, en diden' 'low no wuk on Sundays. No hosses wuz hitched up fer em, en de on'y wuk done wuz jes' milk de cows. De cookin' wuz done Friday en Saturday, but one or two od de slaves what wuked at de cookin' en settin' of de tab-les, had ter kinder stick roun', but got home in time ter go ter meetin'. When dey wuz weddin's, or funerals on holidays, dey wuzn't no wuk done cept jws' what couldn't be got roun' doin'".

"I member all de slaves what cud get out fum de quarters, comin' ter meetin' en de woods ter talk bout gittin way ter freedom er goin off ter war. Some fum our place did go off. Us all knowed de Underground

Railroad t'rough de whole country. Kaze lots of Quakers had come en bought pro-perty on dem parts. en dey wuz a teachin' de slaves ter not be feard of dey rights."

"De folks what owned de next plantation to our'n, de Bigstaffs, wuz cruel ter dey slaves, en some de Bigstaffs boys ud kine de patrollers en help ter ketch slaves en whip em if dey couldn't show a pass fum dey massters."

"I seen em drivin' long lines of slaves chained togedder, with de lit-tle ones pitched up en er ox cart, en I don't know how many men on horseback with long whips slashin' em en drivin' em long de road. Dem slave traders done gone all roun' en bought up men en women some of em right from de fiel'; no time for em ter say good bye ter de fam'lies, buyin' em sellin' em worse'n cattle."

"De slave traders tuk em ter a halfway house on de Tennessee high-way close ter us, own by Billy Wurtz. He had big cellar whar dey put de slaves till dey goin' ter sell em er e'se take em fu'ther south. Dey uster make a big sale day at Mt. Sterling, en auction off de slaves. Dey'd whip em on de block ter make em holler. I seen all dat, em mo'."

"When de war come on lots of de Lane slaves done went in. My father en brother Wash went, en Wash wuz in de battle, 'tween Gin'ral Morgan en Ginral Burden roun' Mt. Sterling."

"Lots of women en chillun went en ter Camp Nelson en lived at what dey called de Woman's Hall. De men what cared ter go dere went ter de bar-racks at Camp Nelson."

"When de war wuz over father en Wash dey both come home. Jim Lane freed us fore de war wuz over, en give us all a little money or paid some ef dey wuz stayin' on till de war wuz over. Dem dat stayed atter de war he give em ten acres of lan' en built em a little place ter live in."

"Us went ter Nicholsville, en wuked roun', some of us on farms. Father done blacksmithin'. Mother saved money fum sellin' chickens en eggs, en pretty soon we had 'nough ter buy en build a nice six-room house. Dat wuz right atter de war."

"Way back dere we used 'lasses ter sweeten mos' ever't'ing, en I member de first sugar we had. It wuz'nt white like it is now, but wuz more like that light brown sugar."

"I lived en Springfield fer 55 years, en I seen a lot of changes,I marriee both my wives her in Springfield. Dey is both daid now. Dey's three of my fam'ly left, two brothers livin' en Cincinnaty, en me here."

I allus been a Methodist en Wiley is my church. I thank de Lawd fer all de blessin's he's 'lowed me ter have."

"I knowed Ben Arnett pu'sonally en heerd him speak lots of times; en too I heard Booker T. Washington en Douglas, en mos' all de big men' mong Negro folks. I read a little, en I done read lots bout mos' of de ones aint heerd."

LUCY ANN WARFIELD
Ex-slave, age said to be 117 years.

"Lordy, chile, I'se been old so long, dat de 'fliction of years mek me fergit lots en lots I mought tell you. I wuz bawn en Jass'min County, Kaintucky, but I caint say what year, kaze white folks diden keep no 'count of dey slaves ages. Dey wuz jes' like chickens- like so many chichens."

"I knows I wuz er married 'oman when de wah come, en dey says I'se more'n a hundred, en Nannie she say I'se about 117. But I jes' doan know. Anyhow, I knows dat God's been awful good ter me."

"My mother wuz Betsy Hawkins, en my father wuz Milo Hawkins. How us come ter have de name of Hawkins, I caint say; kaze de on'y slave owners I knowed wuz Scotts en Perrys. Dey owned all our fam'ly, my grandmother, my mother en father, Mary, Fannie, Sophia, Marcie, Har-vey, Charles en John - Jack dey called him. You see de Scott girl mar-ried en ter de Perry fam'ly, en dey jes give em er lot er slaves, en so all our fam'ly wuz dey property."

"Dey nebber did give me er whippin, but dey sho done wuk me hard. I done er man's wuk on de place; puttin' up stone fences en rail fences, splittin' rails, breakin' hemp, plowin' fiel's, doin' cawn plantin', en eny thing de men spose ter do, en I wuz sposed ter say nothin'. De good vLord an'y knows jes' what I'se been t'rough."

"I member when one of my mother's sisters run of en got safe en ter Canady. she wuz er fine 'oman en she diden keer fer nothin', on'y ter be free. She done what more of em orter done - me, too, kaze I wuz
grown en size long time fore us wuz free- but dey wuz jes'fraid."

"I married to Gilbert Burns fore de wah broke out. He went off ter wah en done come back home safe. Us had one son, little Jesse, but he died when he wuz jes' er little feller."

"When folks got sick dey diden call doctors, cept onct en er while. T'aint no use nobuddy sayin' jes' cullud folks done use herbs, kaze I knows better. White folks done use em same as any buddy else. Dey use ter use catnip tea, horehound, en lots o' roots cut up en put
en whiskey fer use en case of sickness."

"I diden go ter school, but I larnt ter read de Bible. I got me er license fer ter be er 'vangelist. God jes' give me song en words. I sho b'lieve en dat ole song, "Where You Go I'll Go With You; Open
Your Mouth en I'll Speak Fer You," kaze dat's what He's done fer me. I'se been all roun' dese parts preachin' God's words."

"But, honey, back en dem days, when us diden go ter church much, en diden have much 'joyment, but I sho loved dancin', en dat wuz jes' bout all de 'joyment us had. But I larnt Ter praise God harder den I larnt ter serve de debbil, en ef it wuz'nt fer His power I woa'nt be here right now."

"When I moved out here en dis part of town it wuz'nt nothin' but woods. Me en Mr. Warfiel' had er cabin jes' crost de street fum here. Its been tore down fer years, kaze I done live en dis house fer about fifty years. I wisht I cud member more, kaze I been t'rough er lot, abut I doan member nothin' much no more.

"I still sing, "I'm Clim'ing Jacob's Ladder," en I knows I'se goin' ter set down 'sides my Saviour some o' dese days.

<h1 style="text-align:center">VIRGINIA WASHINGTON</h1>
Ex-slave, age estimated as 90

"Fact is, I doan reely know my right age, but I was bawn en slavery times, en I was big ernuff ter wuk when freedom come. I come fum Paris, Tennessee, whar I'se bawn en lived en de home er Benjamin Brown en he's wife Grace."

"Marse Brown he owned my mother en lots er slaves, but when de war broke out, en dey all thought de ud lose all dey slaves when freedom come, why, dey done jes' pack em off down ter Mississippi en sol' em. Some o' de slaves got'er way ter war fore dey cid git er chanct ter sell em."

"I member my mother sayin' she aint nebber goan see me ergin, en she diden'. Dey kep' me, en made me leave de cabin en sleep en de big house, en do de washin', ironin', cookin', fannin' flies offen de table while de white folks et, en slep en er dining room."

"Eben ef I stayed en er house with em, dey diden' wan' me ter eat what det et. Dey mak me eat ole fat meat en cawnbread 'thout no butter ner syrup. Dey give me shoes en wool stockin's fer de winter, but soon as de weather wua hardly warm det tul off dem shoes en made me go bar'footed."

"One day I made up my mind I wuz goin' ter try en git erway, ef I died en doin' it, kaze I done got ter whar I'd ruther be daid den keep on so. Do you know dat hard treatment mek you feel dat way? Ell, I got jes' like dat inside, but I done act sweet en deceitful like."
"One night I seed 'twuz de bes' chanct I'd ebber git, so I les 'slipped er way. I diden' have nothin' cept de close on my back, en not many of em."

"I thought I wuz goan try en mek it up ter Cincinnaty. Islep' in er woods unner bresh heaps fer sev'ral days. Den a bunch of Yankee sojers come past. It wuz er God send, I reckon, kaze dey kep' me en camp fer a few days, en say dey knowed when er boat wuz due en Memphis, en dat dey cud git me off safe with some men dey knowed on de boat."

"I got through all right, en wuz up ter Cincinnaty, at er place whar dey say I'd be safe with folks dey knowed. I reckon Brown's diden' go to a lot of trouble bout me, kaze I nebber heerd no more of em."

"I wuked up en Cincinnaty at cookin' out fer folks. Dat seem ter be bout all dey wuz fer mos' all 'omans ter do, cept washin' en ironin' en, mebbe nursin"."

"Atter de war wuz over, I met up with James Ammett, who'd been off ter de war, en run on er boat up ter Cincinnaty. Us got mar-ried, en had two daughters. Jim he got kill when de boat he wuz wukin' on got blowed up. Den I married Alexander Washington, en now him and both my girls are daid, en nobuddy lef' cept me."

"I tell you, nobuddy kin tell en mek folks b'lieve how some us cullud folks wuz treated by humans, en jes' see, how folks wuz Sol' like p'taters."

"I belongs to Nawth Street Church, en I lived here en Springfield bout thirty five years, I reckon. En I seen lots o' hardships en so much sufferin' en my time."

SALLAH WHITE
Ex-slave, age unknown.

"I jes' cant say how long I been livin', but I wuz er young woman when de war wuz goin' on."

"My grandmother en grandfather, en my mother en five of us chillun wuz owned by Cap'n en Miss Tea Kelly, of Co'win, Tennessee."

"Mother wuz one o' de cooks; grandfather wuz er overseer, en grandmother she wuz er weaver. Dey wuz er weaver fer sure, en right pretty too."

"I wuz raised in de house with de kids of de Kellys. Cap'n Kelly give me ter Miss Tea when she wuz er little girl en I wuz jes' er baby. Dey kep' me en de house, en I slep' unner Miss Tea's bed, en er trunnerl bed. When Miss Tea married en her chillun come along, I wuz de nurse fer em."

"Kellys done teach mos' all dey slaves ter read en write, cept dem what diden' wanna learn."

"I was stole onct en sol' down en Gawgia, ter Alex Hannah. He wuz er slave trader en mean as de debbil he'self. En he had overseers dat ud soon as not kill er man fe he diden' let em whip him."

"I run off fum Hannah's place en got back ter Marse Kelly's, safe. I follered er star what I uster watch come down over Miss Tea' window, en I kin point it out yet. Kelly's slaves nebber wuz whipped by none o' dem patrollers, kaze he diden' 'low none of em whipped."

"I went to de Hardshell Baptist Church with Miss Tea Kelly en Marse Kelly. Dey uster sing er song I nebber aint forgot yet:
'Oh, de Hardshell ship is er moughty good ship; She is safe en sound. Who woan go on de Hardshell ship?
For de Glory Land she's bound.'"

"I kin do der lot o' doctorin', but I woan tell nobuddy what I use; kaze dat is my en god's secret. Folks is sho' b'lievin en all kin's o' conjurs en hoodooin', but dey aint nothin' ter dat debbilment. I b'lieve en carryin' one of Doctor J. C.'s lucky pieces, t'ough, en I'se agent fer em. De doctor he's a Jew, en dem luck
pieces who' will bring you luck. I knos dat, kaze I done had seven law suits, en I win all of em."

"When de war wuz goin' on, us cud hear de roar of de cannons, en Lord! chile, it sho wuz awful. I hate ter talk erbout it."

"Atter freedom, Marse Kelly give all us what stayed on de plan-tation, ten acrew of land en timber ter build us er house. Mother en em stayed on fer five years atter freedom, en den went ter Owens-boro', Tennessee. En now here I am en Springfiel', fer 24 years. All six er my chillun en ly husban', dey is all daid, en I am stillhere, ter tell you all tales o' de times I'se come t'rough."

"Uncle Marion fum Kelly's place went ter Jasper, Tennessee, atter freedom, en de done open er school. Uncle Marion had er fair eddycation en he got erlong well 'nough teachin'. Schools dey jus' sprung up, all t'rough de south atter freedom; fer so many nawth'n folks come down en open up schools. I'se tellin' you, dem poor, cullud folks dey needed it, too kaze dey's allus been kep' back so, en nebber wuz give no chance.

DAVID WILBORN
Ex-slave, age 81

"I was bawn in Athens, Gawgia, Jan.13, 1856. My father, Robert Wilborn was a Cherokee Indian. My mother was the daughter of a Negro woman and a German doctor. There were fifteen child'un of us, twelve boys and three girls. Dr. Edward Ware owned mother and we child'un, and father worked for him, making coffins for use when any of the slaves on his plantation died, and for Dr. Ware to sell, too."

"Dr. Ware owned a large numbuh of slaves - I jes' dont know how many, but I heard mother say they was something like a hundred. He was the doctor that examined the slaves for the auction, and he was a slave trader.

"Father died in 1863. I remembuh he was buried in one of the coffins he made himself. It was put on a wagon pulled by a mule. A man led the mule and our family walked down the road behind the wagon to the cemetery."
"Of co'se we lived in a cabin. That was the way all slaves lived. We ate cawn bread and fat meat, and hardly any vegetables, and syrup. We went barefoot, and wore loose shirts with a hole, cut for the haid to go through, and a hole for each arm. Many a day I picked cotton from sunrise to dark when I was jes' a little fellow."

"I remembuh our old Missus having a big hole or underground tunnel dug so they could hide their hosses. The tunnel was lined with boards, and the hosses put down in it, and then they covered up the hole. But the Union soldiers was used to that way of hiding cattle and hosses, so of co'se they found em."

"Old Missus cried and said, 'You can help yourself to the strawberries, but please dont take my nice carriage hosses,' It made the soldiers laugh.

They took the hosses, and helped themselves to the strawberries and any-thing else they wanted, anyway."

"Aftuh freedom we stayed on the Ware plantation till 1869. One of my older brothers went to Augusta and was working in a hotel, and he sent for the rest of us to come. Some of my brothers and sisters had been sold off into slavery, and mother could'nt locate em again. She took what was left of we child'un and refugeed to Atlanta, and got herself a job with a family named Dennick. Mother was a very good cook, and she stayed with this family
till she died, in 1874."

"I went to school for a while, but the facilities was poor, and I did'nt have money for books; so I stopped and went to work in the field picking cotton. Teachers come into the South aftuh the wah like missionaries. Most of em was from Massachusetts, Vermont and New York."

"I left Augusta and went to Look Out Mountain where I worked in a hotel. Then I come to Yellow Springs, Ohio, and worked with, my brother John in a hotel there. That was about 65 years ago."

"I come to Springfield 63 years ago and begun work in the Lagonda Hotel. I learned to read and write by the traveling men who come to the hotel. But I read all I had time to read and used a dictionary all the time."

"I represented the Negroes of Springfield as their correspondent in the following papers: The Cleveland Gazette; The voice of the People; The Lexing-ton Herald; The Detroit Plaindealer; The Christian Recorder of Philadelphia, which Bishop Lee was editor of; and the Indianapolis Freeman."

CLARK HEARD
Ex-Slave 86 years

Although born in August, 1851, Clark Heard insists he was but nine years old at the close of the Civil War.

While he puffed on a villainous pipe, he was persuaded at length togive to posterity the following facts of his slavehood:

"I was born in August, 1851, on a 300-acre plantation in Troup County, Georgia. De plantation was five mile from Wes' Point an' jes' twelve mile from La Grange -- dat's de county seat of Troup County.

My father was Amos Heard, born in Charleston, South Carolina. Don' know what my mother, Delilah, was born -- somewhar in Virginny.

Dar was seven of us boys and one gal, Katie Saphonia -- or Saphonia Katie -- it's jes' a same either way.

Oldes' boy was Hardy; nex', George Washington; nex', Whit -- don't know if it was Whitman or not, we jes' call 'im Whit; nex', myself, Clark; nex', Pascall; nex', Edgah; nex', Willis.

De Marzer was Jesse Palmer, an' he shuh was good to all us colored folk. I never worked until Surrender. Yes. Surrender. Yo' know, don' yo', dat's what dey call it wen dey was freed. I never worked while on Marse Jesse's place 'cause he didn' work his boys until dey'd nine, an' I was jes' nine at Surrender.

My gran'father was Henry Heard. He wasn't a real slave. He was a stage driver. You know what a stage be? Oh yes, every plantation had one -- some had two or three.

My father was a fine carpenter an' a fine blacksmith, an' my gran'father used to give him work to do an' he'd pay my father. What did he buy with the money? Nuthin'. Dere was no need to buy. Our Marzer see to it dat we have everything we need. My father he save all de money, but it didn't do him any good 'cause Surrender spoil all de Confederate money. Shuh, I see all kin's of money. We had 'bout two bushels Confederate pennies, but dey don' do us any, good. My father, he was smart -- he could do anything. Why, he cut de iron for the fus' bridge ever put up in Georgia -- he an' a man in La Grange were togedder in de business.

Yes, ma'am, we had all de eatin' we could want -- milk an' butter an' syrup. My Marzer he start in Augus' makin' syrup, an' he never stop until January. Corn? Nawl Great big ribs of cane big as my arm. No, we didn't have separate gardens. De Marzer he had 15 to 25 acres of garden an' hiscolored folk dey have plenty.

Some was mean, though. On de nex' plantation dat Billy Cotton he was mean, I tell yo'. He had 'bout 300 people an' he give 'em pone an' nuthin' much more, an' he work 'em in de' fiel' from sunup to-- sundown, den he make 'em. work till 11 o'clock at night spinnin' silk from de worms he had -- dose worms come from Englan' -- das why he's so rich. He was jes' plain bad, an' he'd whip an' whip his people. He'd git 'em up at, four in de morning to whip 'em. But he was fixed at Surrender. Dose Yankee sojers dey done him bad, I tell you, cause dey hear he's so mean to his people. Dey hang him up by his thumbs an' make him tell whar all his money is, an' dey took it, an' all his silver an' blankets an' everything. An' dey take all his fine hosses, 'bout 50 or 75. Dat Billy Cotton he have some of de fines' hosses you ever did see, an' dey take everyone o' dem.

No, de sojers didn't take anything from Marse Jesse 'cause he good.

Paddyrollers? Marse Jesse he not allow a paddyroller or overseer on de plantation. He did all dat hisself. Ef dey war any whippin' to be done Marze Jesse he did it, but mos' times he punish in some other way, jes' like white folks punish dere chillun.

My mother she raise sixteen chillun -- eight of her own an' eight of de Marzer's. She was a house girl. She did de cookin' an' she take keer of de Marzer's chillun, Sometime she nurse de Marser's chillun. Dey call her Black Mammy an' dey jes' love her. Wherever dey see her dey hug an' kiss her. She weave all de clothes on big looms. Dere was jes' her an' another
girl in de house. All de other slaves, maybe 140 to 150, 'was in de fiel'.

Yes, ma'am, we had plenty o' possum an' rabbit. I has two fice,blacker den I am, an' dey ketch dat possum every time. Fice? Dogs dey was, but I calls 'em fice.

We had red shoes. Yes, ma'am, dey was red. Dey'd tan de leather an'it ud turn red, an' nobody bother to make it black. Both blacks an' whites dey wear dose red shoes. Clothes? We wore some kin' of cotton. It was
white an' we had to keep it clean, I tell yo'.

Shuh, dey was plenty of poor whites. Sometime dey was overseers but not on our place. But wen things git busy sometime Marzer he puts 'em to work in de fiel', only dey get money an' we don'.

Marzer Jesse he was a preacher, an' he was good, too. He preach at de Big Bethel Church, an' we all. had to go.

Shuh, we was sen', to school. Billy Hogg built a school on his place an' dey hired Jim Farnham to teach us. Yo' know, de Union dey cause dat war. Dey 'fraid de South she have de mos' money an' people an' come up an' take de North, an' dey deman' de South it come into de Union, or dey come down after it. Abraham Lincoln he say he make 'em water dere hosses in Lake Erie of dey don', an' he did, too. Dat was a war, I tell yo'. In dese other wars dey jes' use guns, an' airplanes, an' sech, but I tell yo' dat was four years of real fightin' wi flint an' shot gun. I see cannon ball 'bout de size of my fis'. Yes, ma'am, dat was a war."

At this point, the mother and several youngsters of the family with whom Clark lives, had an attack of hunger so they deserted the audience chamber and gathered around the kitchen table, in full view of Clark's persistently turned face. With a finality that left no opening for further questions, Clark indicated that the interview was over.

The big, rather good-looking colored woman with whom he lives volubly elucidated Clark's peculiar temperament, "He look jes' like a man but he no man. He jes' a little boy like my own little boys an' I have to treat him like a little boy. He get to fightin' wi' my boys 'bout marbles, an' he say, 'Dose my marbles, an' de chillun dey say, No, dose not his marbles,'" and she sighed at the great amount of responsibility an old-boy of Clark's temperament involved. "But he's jes' dat nice. He allus say, 'Yes, ma'am,' an' 'No, ma'am.'

Charity Anderson
Mobile, Alabama

Interviewed by Ila B. Prine

She said "Missy, peoples don't live now, and niggers ain't got no manners, and don't know nothin' about waitin' on white folks. I kin remember de days when I was one of de house servants. Dere was six of us in de ol' marster's house, me, Sarai, Lou, Hester, Jerry and Joe. Us didn't know nothin' but good times den. My job was lookin' a'ter de corner table whar nothin' but de desserts sat. Jo and Jerry were de table boys, and dey ne'ber touched nothin' wid dere hans', dey used de waiter to pass things wid. My! dem was good ol' days.

"My old Marster was a good man, he treated all his slaves kind, and took care of dem, he wanted to leave dem hisn chillun. It sho' was hard for us older uns to keep de little cullered chillun out ob de dinin' room whar ol marster ate, cause when dey would slip in and stan' by his cheer, when he finished eatin' he would fix a plate and gib dem and dey would set on de hearth and eat. But honey chile, all white folks warn 't good to dere slaves, cause I'se seen pore niggers almos' tore up by dogs, and whipped unmercifully, when dey did'nt do lack de white folks say . But thank God I had good white folks, dey sho' did trus' me to, I had charge of all de keys in the house and I waited on de Missy and de chillun. I laid out all dey clos' on Sat 'dy night on de cheers, and den Sund'y mawnings I'd pick up all de dirty clos', they did'nt have to do a thing. And as for working in the field, my marster neber planted no cotton, I neber seed no cotton planted til' a'ter I was free.

"But listen, honey, I sho' could wash, iron, knit and weave, bless yuh, I could finish my days' work aroun' de house, and den weave six or seven yards o'cloth. I'se washed, ironed and waited on de fourth generation ob dis family. I l'arned de chillun how to wash, iron, weave, and knit. I jes wish I could tell dese young chillun how to do, if dey would only suffer me to talk to dem, I'd tell dem to be more 'spectful to dere mammas, and to dere white folks and say 'yes mam' an 'no mam', instid of 'yes' and 'no' lack dey do now.

"I ain't neber been in no tr'uble in mah life, I ain't been in no lawsuits, I ain't neber been no witness. I neber had seen a show in my life 'til jes dis pas' year, when a show, wid swings, lights, and all de doings dey have stop' in front ob our house har.

"I'se allus tried to treat eberybody as good as I kin, and I uses my manners as good as I knows how, and de Lord sho' has taken keer ob me. Why, when my house burnt up, de white folks helped me so dat in no time you could'nt tell I had ebber los' a thing.

But honey, de good ol' days is don' gone forebber. Bless you when we lib at Johnson's Landing on de river, folks would come dere to catch de steamboats, and we neber knowed how many to put on breakfas, dinner, or supper fo' cause sometimes de boats would be a little behin' times and sometimes a little before times and we allus had a house full. And as for paying my fare on de boats, I neber had dat to do, when ole Captain John Quill wars livin' he allus lowed me to ride his boat fo' nothin anywhar I wanted to go. But what's the use thinking about dem times, dey's gone, and de world is 'gettin' wicked'er, sin is bolder and bolder, and religion grows colder and colder".

Tempe Herndon Durham
Durham, North Carolina
Interviewed by Travis Jordan

"I was thirty-one years ole when de surrender come. Dat makes me sho nuff ole. Near bout a hundred an' three years done passed over dis here white head of mine. I'se been here, I mean I'se been here. 'Spects I'se de oldest nigger in Durham. I'se been here so long dat I done forgot near 'bout as much as dese here new generation knows or ever gwine know.

My white fo'ks lived in Chatham County. Dey was Marse George an' Mis' Betsy Herndon. Mis Betsy was a Snipes befo' she married Marse George. Dey had a big plantation an' raised cawn, wheat, cotton an' 'bacca. I don't know how many field niggers Marse George had, but he had a mess of dem, an' he had hosses too, an' cows, hogs an' sheeps. He raised sheeps an' sold de wool, an' dey used de wool at de big house too. Dey was a big weavin' room whare de blankets was wove, an' dey wove de cloth for de winter clothes too. Linda Hernton an' Milla Edwards was de head weavers, dey looked after de weavin' of da fancy blankets. Mis' Betsy was a good weaver too. She weave de same as de niggers. She say she love de clackin' soun' of de loom an' de way de shuttles run in an' out carryin' a long tail of bright colored thread. Some days she set at de loom all de mawnin' peddlin' wid her feets an' her white han's flittin' over de bobbins.

De cardin' an' spinnin' room was full of niggers. I can hear dem spinnin' wheels now turnin' roun' an' sayin' hum-m-m-m, hum-m-m-m, an' hear de slaves singin' while dey spin. Mammy Rachel stayed in de dyein' room. Dey wuzn' nothin' she didn' know 'bout dyein'. She knew every kind of root, bark, leaf an' berry dat made red, blue, green, or whatever color she wanted. Dey had a big shelter whare de dye pots set over de coals. Mammy Rachel would fill de pots wid water, den she put in de roots, bank an' stuff an' boil de juice out, den she strain it an' put in de salt an' vinegar to set de color. After de wool an' cotton done been carded an' spun to thread, Mammy take de hanks an' drap dem in de pot of boilin' dye. She stir dem 'roun' an' lif' dem up an' down wid a stick, an' when she hang dem up on de line in de sun, dey was every color of de rainbow. When dey dripped dry dey was sent to de weavin' room whare dey was wove in blankets an' things.
When I growed up I married Exter Durham. He belonged to Marse Snipes Durham who had de plantation 'cross de county line in Orange County. We had a big weddin'. We was married on de front po'ch of de big house. Marse George killed a shoat an' Mis' Betsy had Georgianna, de cook, to bake a big weddin' cake all iced up white as snow wid a bride an' groom standin' in de middle holdin' han's. De table was set out in de yard under de trees, an' you ain't never seed de like of eats.
All de niggers come to de feas' an' Marse George had a for everybody. Dat was some weddin'. I had on a white dress, white shoes an' long while gloves dat come to my elbow, an' Mis' Betsy done made me a weddin' veil out of a white net window curtain. When she played de weddin' ma'ch on de piano, me an' Exter ma'ched down de walk an' up on de po'ch to de altar Mis' Betsy done fixed. Dat de pretties' altar I ever seed. Back 'gainst de rose vine dat was full or red roses, Mis' Betsy done put tables filled wid flowers an' white candles.

She spread down a bed sheet, a sho nuff linen sheet, for us to stan' on, an' dey was a white pillow to kneel down on. Exter done made me a weddin' ring. He made it out of a big red button wid his pocket knife. He done cut it so roun' an' polished it so smooth dat it looked like a red satin ribbon tide 'roun' my finger.

Dat sho was a pretty ring. I wore it 'bout fifty years, den it got so thin dat I lost it one day in de wash tub when I was washin' clothes.

Uncle Edmond Kirby married us. He was de nigger preacher dat preached at de plantation church. After Uncle Edmond said de las' words over me an' Exter, Marse George got to have his little fun: He say, 'Come on, Exter, you an' Tempie got to jump over de broom stick backwards; you got to do dat to see which one gwine be boss of your househol'.' Everybody come stan' 'roun to watch. Marse George hold de broom 'bout a foot high off de floor. De one dat jump over it backwards an' never touch de handle, gwine boss de house, an' if bof of dem jump over widout touchin' it, dey won't gwine be no bossin', dey jus' gwine be 'genial. I jumped fus', an' you ought to seed me. I sailed right over dat broom stick same as a cricket, but when Exter jump he done had a big dram an' his feets was so big an' clumsy dat dey got all tangled up in dat broom an' he fell head long. Marse George he laugh an' laugh, an' tole Exter he gwine be bossed 'twell he skeered to speak less'n I tole him to speak. After de weddin' we went down to de cabin Mis' Betsy done all dressed up, but Exter couldn' stay no longer den dat night kaze he belonged to Marse Snipes Durham an' he had to go back home. He lef' de nex day for his plantation, but he come back every Saturday night an' stay 'twell Sunday night. We had eleven chillun. Nine was bawn befo' surrender an' two after we was set free. So I had two chillun dat wuzn' bawn in bondage. I was worth a heap to Marse George kaze I had so many chillun. De more chillun a slave had de more dey was worth. Lucy Carter was de only nigger on de plantation dat had more chillun den I had. She had twelve, but her chillun was sickly an' mine was muley strong an' healthy. Dey never was sick.

When de war come Marse George was too ole to go, but young Marse Bill went. He went an' took my brother Sim wid him. Marse Bill took Sim along to look after his hoss an' everything. Dey didn' neither one get shot, but Mis' Betsy was skeered near 'bout to death all de time, skeered dey was gwine be brung home shot all to pieces like some of de sojers was.

(De Yankees wuzn' so bad. De mos' dey wanted was sumpin' to eat. Dey was all de time hungry, de fus' thing dey ax for when dey come was sumpin' to put in dey stomach. An' chicken! I ain' never seed even a preacher eat chicken like dem Yankees. I believes to my soul dey ain' never seed no chicken 'twell dey come down here. An' hot biscuit too. I seed a passel of dem eat up a whole sack of flour one night for supper. Georgianna sif' flour 'twell she look white an' dusty as a miller. Dem sojers didn' turn down no ham neither. Dat de onlies' thing dey took from Marse George. Dey went in de smoke house an' toted off de hams an' shoulders. Marse George say he come off mighty light if dat all dey want, 'sides he got plenty of shoats anyhow.

We had all de eats we wanted while de war was shootin' dem guns, kaze Marse George was home an' he kep' de niggers workin'. We had chicken, gooses, meat, peas, flour, meal, potatoes an' things like dat all de time, an' milk an' butter too, but we didn' have no sugar an' coffee. We used groun' pa'ched cawn for coffee an' cane 'lasses for sweetnin'. Dat wuzn' so bad wid a heap of thick cream. Anyhow, we had enough to eat to 'vide wid de neighbors dat didn' have none when surrender come.

I was glad when de was stopped kaze den me an' Exter could be together all de time 'stead of Saturday an' Sunday. After we was free we lived right on at Marse George's plantation a long time. We rented de lan' for a fo'th of what we made, den after while we bought a farm. We paid three hundred dollars we done saved. We had a hoss, a steer, a cow an' two pigs, 'sides some chickens an' fo' geese. Mis' Betsy went up in de attic an' give us enough goose feathers to make two pillows, den she give us a table an' some chairs. She give us some dishes too. Marse George give Exter a bushel of seed cawn and some seed wheat, den he tole him to go down to de barn an' get a bag of cotton seed. We got all dis den we hitched up de wagon an' th'owed in de passel of chillun an' moved to our new farm, an' de chillun was put to work in de fiel'; dey growed up in de fiel' kaze dey was put to work time dey could walk good.

Freedom is all right, but de niggers was better off befo' surrender, kaze den dey was looked after an' dey didn' get in no trouble fightin' an' killin' like dey do dese days. If a nigger cut up an' got sassy in slavery times, his Ole Marse give him a good whippin' an' he went way back an' set down an' 'haved hese'f. If he was sick, Marse an' Mistis looked after him, an' if he needed store medicine, it was bought an' give to him; he didn' have to pay nothin'. Dey didn' even have to think 'bout clothes nor nothin' like dat, dey was wove an' made an' give to dem. Maybe everybody's Marse and Mistis wuzn' good as Marse George and Mis' Betsy, but dey was de same as a mammy an' pappy to us niggers."

Rose Holman
Age about 84

"I was born near Greensboro in what was then Choctaw county. My mama was Millie Drain an' I had a outside papa. (He was Bob Jones.) My mama had several chillen born to her but me an' my brother Anderson Drain is the only ones living now. Anderson, he jus' ten years younger 'n me. I 'member he born de year befo' de war ceasted. I was nursin' him when we was freed. They tells me I was ten years old then an' that's all I knows 'bout my age."

"We lived in little log houses dobbed wid mud an' didn't have no beds--slept on de ground on pallets. We eat out o' troughs down at Marsa's back doo' an et wid muscle shells fo' spoons."

"My Mama an' her sister Cenie was sold. Mama used to slip back at night an' bring us things an' de white folks never knowed it. It sho' would-a went hard wid her if dey'd ever caught her."

"My job durin' slavery days was toatin' water an' pickin' up chips. I wasn't like de other little niggers--my head wasn't flat on top an' old Missus saw I couldn't tote nothin' on my head. Other niggers could bring a bucket o' water on their head an' one in each hand. I was allus a sickly baby. My guts come down in my navel an' I never was well 'till I got grown. When I was a little baby Mama used to leave me in de cabin by my self fo' hours at a time. Old Miss tell Mama: "Go down to dat house an' see if dat little nigger aint dead." They said I was allus a good baby."

"Old Miss sho' had a time wid me an' her little chickens. I jus' loved little chickens to death. I 'member she wouldn't let me round 'em cause she'd 'fraid I'd hurt em an' one day I slipped off in de woods where de old hen an' her bunch was. I caught every one of em an' bit their heads off. Dat old hen fought me 'till my face was covered in blood when I got to de house."

"Mama never did 'low us to dance. I never did 'low my chillen to dance either. I 'member gettin' off one time an' tryin' to dance when they wasn't nobody 'round an' stumped my toe. It broke me tho'. I never did try it no mo. I sho like to broke my toe tho'."

"I 'member hearin' my nigger women say: "So glad I's free! So glad I's free!" De war was over an' they didn't have no boss. I 'member Mama tellin' 'bout de Yankees cuttin' de cloth out de loom an' gettin' up on it with their horses. They took de feather beds an' throwed 'em way but after they was gone we found em."

"Mama said she had a better time in slavery days then after they was freed. She was a house girl. I's heard some hollowin': "Oh pray Mistus." Law me, dey would be gettin' some whippin'. These women dat didn't work in de field sho' had their four rolls to spin a day. Mama said she'd allus get hers--sometime she'd finish at night but heep o' de women had to have a whippin' 'fore theirs was done an' then they'd sho' get busy."

"I was 18 years old when I married Charlie Holman an' he was even 21. My weddin' dress was made out of' dis swiss cloth an' trimmed in blue ribbon. I wore a bow on my head an' had a big bow 'round my waist. My, I thought I was steppin' out! We lived in de Tom Holman place in Choctaw county. I don't know 'xactley how long we lived there but we stayed in Louisiana eight years. I tells em dat was de hottest place I ever seen. De buds start swellin' in de spring an' de women start swellin' too. More babies there 'n I ever seen. Dis summer I'd be settin' in de corner great big an next summer I'd be settin' in de corner great big again. I's de mother o' eighteen an' ain't got but three now. De Lord sho' saw fit to take 'em. I was jus' a good breeder. I liked livin' in Louisiana 'cept I jus' didn't like havin' so many chillen. We moved out there in a ox wagon an' it took three weeks to move there. Had a good old dog stayed wid us an' kept de boogers off on de trip. When we moved back we come on de train. When we got back from Louisiana we moved over in Webster county, near Eupora wid Mr. Estel Bridges an' we's been 'round here ever since."

"I belong to de Baptist church. Didn't join 'till I's plum grown. I knowed what I was doin'. We's all got to be regenerated an' born again befo' we leaves dis old world. I tell you de old Time Religion is de best kind o' ligion."

"I tells you they's somethin' behind all dese geese dats gone over dis fall. Dat sho' means bad weather ahead. I can tell de young folks when its gon-a rain. My Rheumatism start hurtin' me den it's sho' to rain."

Advertisements & Photos

Runaway in Jail.

Was brought to the Jail of this parish a runaway negro who calls his name TOM and says he belongs to a Mr. Pomfrey, residing in the parish of St. Mary; said negro is about 26 years of age, 5 feet 8 inches high, and a griffe. The owner will please come forward, pay charges, and take him away. He was taken from on board the steamer Oglesby.

dec12   HENRY SULLIVAN, Jailor.

Marron en Prison.

IL a été amené à la geole de Plaquemine, un nègre arreté comme marron, nommé TOM, et qui se dit appartenir à Mr. Pomfrey, résidant en la paroisse de St. Mary; le dit nègre est agé d'environ 26 ans, 5 pieds 8 pouces de taille.

dec12   HENRY SULLIVAN, Geolier.

Runaway in Jail.

Was brought to the Jail of this Parish a runaway negro who calls his name ALIE, and says he belongs to Henry Doyle, residing in

Southern Sentinel (Plaquemine, LA), December 19, 1849, p. 1

South Carolina and American General Gazette (Charleston), June 12, 1769

25,

TO BE SOLD on Thursday next, at publick vendue,
TEN LIKELY
GOLD COAST NEW NEGROES,
Juft imported from the Weft-Indies,
Confifting of eight ftout men and two women.
To prevent their receiving the infection of
the fmallpox, they have been kept conftantly
on board the veffel fince they arrived, where
they will be fold.—Any perfon inclining to
purchafe them at private fale may apply to Meffrs. Johnfon
and Wylly.

RUN AWAY from the fubfcriber, a NE-
GROE MAN named FRANK, who car-
ried off a gun and fhot pouch with him. He
is a likely well made ftout fellow, fpeaks broken Englifh, with the Spanifh accent, having
been feveral years at the Havana.—Whoever
will deliver him to Mr. George Baillie in Savannah, or to me in Augufta, fhall receive 20s. reward, be-
fides all charges.   JAMES GRAY.

Runaway

FROM the subscriber near Clinton,
Greene county Ala., my negro boy named
FAGANS, who is heavy built, about five
feet eight or ten inches high, near thirty
five years old, has a heavy black beard,
large and long forehead, thin visage, a remarkable long sharp nose, and having lost
one of his front teeth. Any person who will catch
the above described boy, and return him or give us
any information, shall be liberally rewarded.
                              Wm. B. BOYKIN.
August 4th, 1838.—4–4w.

"Runaway," Columbus Democrat (Columbus, MS), August 18, 1838, p. 4.

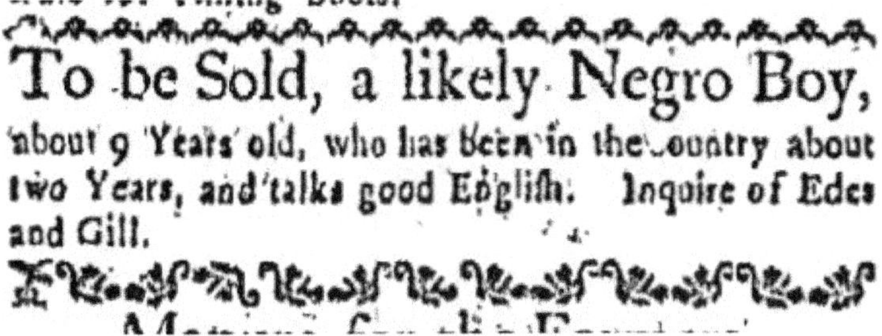

Supplement to the Boston-Gazette (March 16, 1767).

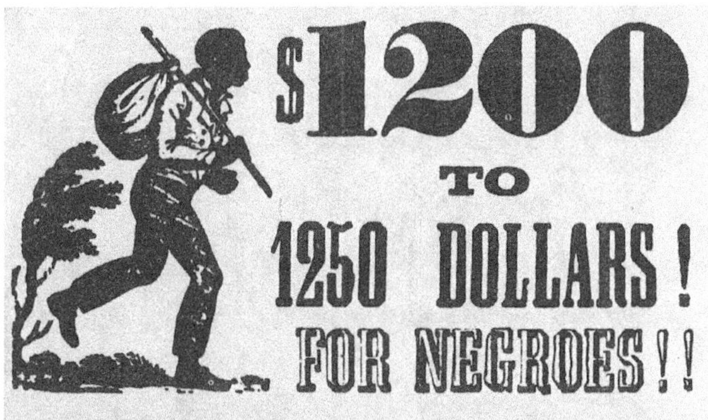

Louisville Kentucky, 1838- Library of Congress

TWENTY DOLLARS REWARD.

RAN AWAY from the plantation of the subscriber, lying in Warren County, ten miles from Vicksburg, some time in February last, a Negro Boy, named

PETER,

about 18 or 20 years of age. five feet seven or eight inches high, well proportioned in make, very active and sprightly; has a pleasing countenance, smiles when spoken to, and is very intelligent; slightly inclined to the mulatto in color, and has a scar on his face, but not recollected where. He took with him several articles of clothing, amongst which was a coat of Kentucky junes that reached to his feet, or nearly so. Said boy was taken up in March last by Charles Cox, near the mouth of Cole's creek, from whom he made his escape, and has not been heard of from that time to the present.

Peter was brought to this state by Franklin and Ballard, last fall, of whom I purchased him. There is no doubt but that he has denied his own as well as his owner's name; if so, he is easily frightened by the whip, and may be made to tell the truth readily. I will give the above reward of twenty dollars to any person delivering said boy to me, or securing him in any jail, so that I can get him again.

P. NOLAND.

Near Rodney, May 27.　　　16–tf

☞ The *Natchez Courier* will please insert the above *three* times, and forward account to this office.

Southern Telegraph (Rodney, MS), August 9, 1836, p. 6.

NEGROES AT AUCTION.—BY J. & L. T. LEVIN.

Will be sold, on Monday, the 3d January next, at the Court House, at 10 o'clock,

22 LIKELY NEGROES, the larger number of which are young and desirable. Among them are Field Hands, Hostlers and Carriage Drivers, House Servants, &c., and of the following ages: Robinson 40, Elsey 34, Yanaky 13, Sylla 11, Anikee 8, Robinson 6, Candy 3, Infant 9, Thomas 35, Die 38, Amey 18, Eldridge 13, Charles 6, Sarah 60, Baket 50, Mary 18, Betty 16, Guy 12, Tilla 9, Lydia 24, Rachel 4, Scipio 2.

The above Negroes are sold for the purpose of making some other investment of the proceeds; the sale will, therefore, be positive.

Terms. — A credit of one, two, and three years, for notes payable at either of the Banks, with two or more approved endorsers, with interest from date. Purchasers to pay for papers. Dec 8 43

☞ *Black River Watchman* will copy the above, and forward bill to the auctioneers for payment.

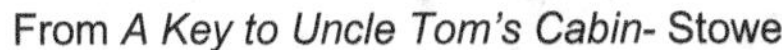

From *A Key to Uncle Tom's Cabin*- Stowe

Barnard, George N, photographer. "Auction & Negro Sales," Whitehall Street. Photograph. Retrieved from the Library of Congress, 1864

Slave Quarters in Savannah
Detroit Publishing Co., Publisher. The Hermitage, slave quarters, Savannah, Ga. [?]
Photograph. Retrieved from the Library of Congress

Gibson, James F, photographer. Cumberland Landing, Va. Group of "contrabands" at Foller's
house. Photograph. Retrieved from the Library of Congress

Houghton, G. H. , Approximately, photographer. Family of slaves at the Gaines' house. [Hanover County, Virginia] Photograph. Retrieved from the Library of Congress

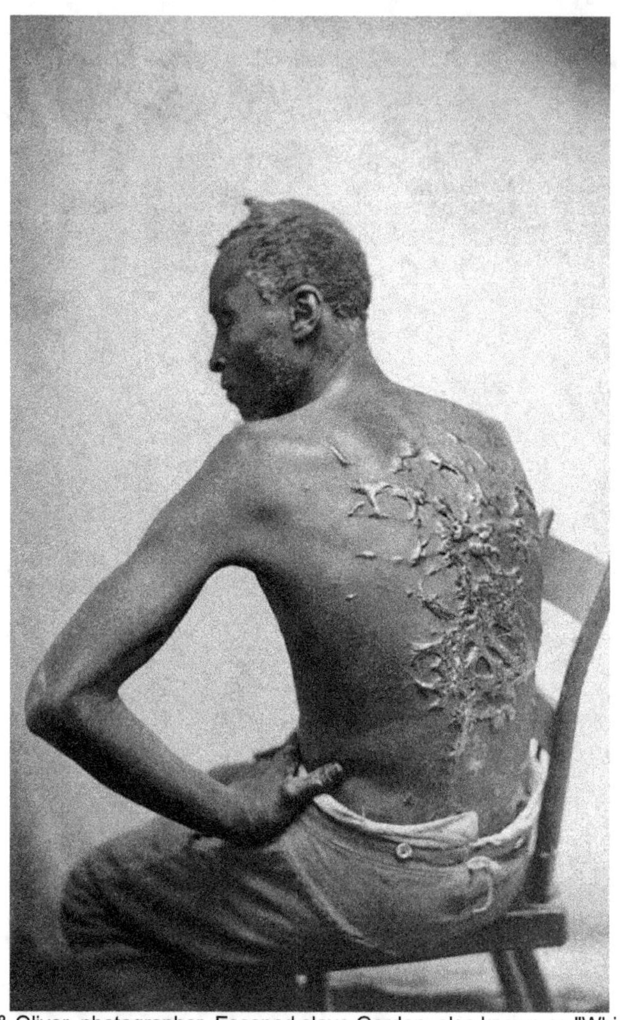

Mcpherson & Oliver, photographer. Escaped slave Gordon, also known as "Whipped Peter," showing his scarred back at a medical examination, Baton Rouge, Louisiana. [Baton Rouge, La.: Publisher not identified, 2 April] Photograph. Retrieved from the Library of Congress

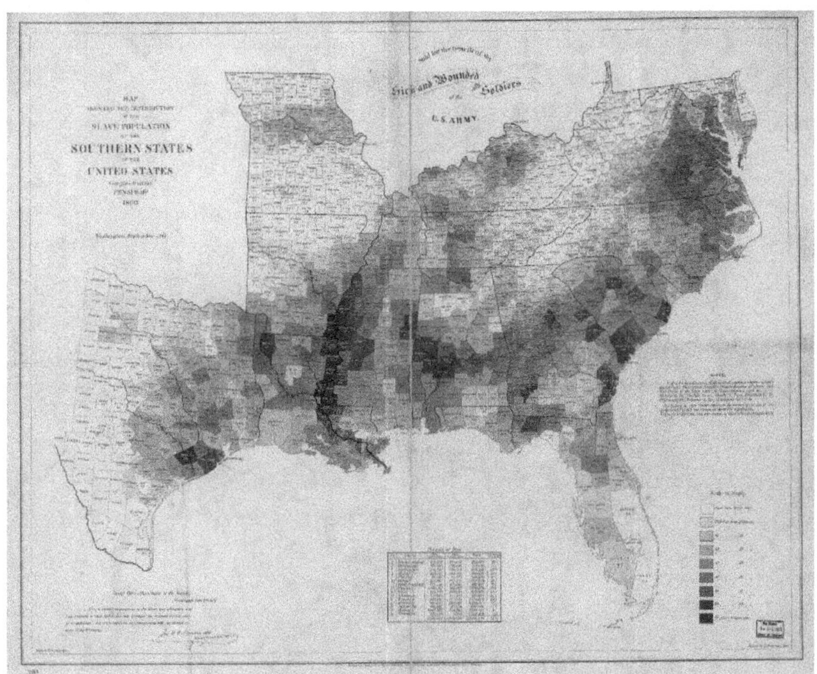

Hergesheimer, E. Map showing the distribution of the slave population of the southern states of the United States. Compiled from the census of. Washington Henry S. Graham, 1861. Map. Retrieved from the Library of Congress

Wilson Chinn, a branded slave from Louisiana--Also exhibiting instruments of torture used to punish slaves. Photograph. Retrieved from the Library of Congress